HARVARD MIDDLE EASTERN MONOGRAPHS

VI

BUARIJ
PORTRAIT OF A LEBANESE MUSLIM VILLAGE

BY

ANNE H. FULLER

DISTRIBUTED FOR THE
CENTER FOR MIDDLE EASTERN STUDIES
OF HARVARD UNIVERSITY BY
HARVARD UNIVERSITY PRESS

CAMBRIDGE, MASSACHUSETTS
1963

PREFACE

The year 1937-38 I spent in the Lebanese village of Buarij. At that time Lebanon was a mandate territory under the control of France. Through Salah Hibri, a student of the American University of Beirut, I was introduced to the village. His family from Beirut owned land in Buarij and also two houses where they had spent the summers for some years. Since the Arab world is a world of personal relations, this personal introduction facilitated my stay. To him and his family I wish to express my indebtedness and thanks.

Though the villagers were accustomed to the few Beirut Muslim summer people who stayed in Buarij, no foreigner had before resided in the community. But since foreigners summer in villages on the opposite western slopes of the Lebanon range overlooking the Mediterranean Sea, the notion of a resident foreigner was not entirely without precedent.

At first I told the villagers that I was merely summering in the village, preferring it to others because of its superior spring water, high location, and commanding view. As I prolonged my stay I frankly said it was because of my interest in their village, their village life, and village ways. First, I came to know village families near at hand, spending most of my time with the women. Through these families I came to know their relatives and neighbors, spending much time in homes, going into the fields with groups, or accompanying them to neighboring towns, to the water mill on the plain below, or to distant villages from which wives had come into Buarij. In the winter of the year many days were spent with herdsmen families who had gone to the coast land, they sharing their food with me in front of their herdsmen's caves and huts.

Information was collected largely by an informal rather than a formal method — by listening to village talk and participating in village affairs. By this means, I was accepted more readily, since the villagers tended to associate direct questions, especially involving statistics or any numerical data, with the unpopular tax collector or other official intruders from outside the village world. All village persons I came to call by kinship terms. The girls were "sisters," the boys "brothers," the grown men "paternal uncles," and the elders "grandfather" and "grandmother." In turn I was treated almost as kin. Living within the community, I adhered to those dictates governing the deportment of an unmarried Muslim woman. From the villagers, increasing loyalty was received. Towards them, I had equal loyalty.

In 1945 during World War II, I managed to return for a day to the village. Meanwhile, the British had evicted the Vichy French from the country. On the main Beirut-Damascus highway were pillboxes and entrenchments. But the village itself had remained untouched. The villagers, however, were full of war talk. From their high location they had witnessed air battles above the plain and the passing of troops, both British and Vichy French, on the main routes of communication. But they themselves had not fared badly. There had been construction work on the roads, and the British had taken over large areas of the plain below for the growing of foods for their troops in the Middle East theater. This had given village men increasing work.

The village men at this time were more adequately clothed than in 1937, largely in British army goods. They said they came by these through means best known to themselves. Because the villagers had been cut off from the towns and from itinerant peddlers, there was a marked revival in certain village crafts, particularly in the spinning and knitting of village wool. But Buarij in its physical appearance remained much the same.

It was in political consciousness that the village had changed most. Lebanon's freedom as an independent nation had been proclaimed. The young men talked much of the future of the country and of the larger Arab setting. The former watchman of the village, a forceful figure, was now a gardener at the American Legation in Beirut. The best place for work was in the cities, he said. But he would return to the village for the summer months. The women as before remained concerned largely with events near at hand. They regretted that they and others from the neighboring villages had not attended the spring festival, badly disrupted by the war years.

From a pair of army trousers hanging on the wall of a house, the legs knotted to form a sack, walnuts were given me. Two eggs were fried in sheep's fat. Later, I turned down the village road towards the highway. Since then I have not seen the peasants of Buarij, who were my friends and whom I came to hold in loyal affection.

To the American Association of University Women I wish to express my thanks for the grant of the Margaret E. Maltby Fellowship which made my stay in the village possible. To the American University of Beirut I owe a debt of gratitude for its friendly and helpful interest and for the use of its library and other facilities. To the Center for Middle Eastern Studies at Harvard University and to its Director, Professor H. A. R. Gibb, I wish to express my thanks for interest and valuable help in the preparation of the manuscript. To Mr. D. W. Lockard, Associate Director of the Center for Middle Eastern Studies, and to Dr. Jane Philips of the Graduate School of Public Health of the University of Pittsburgh, I owe a special debt of gratitude for their friendly understanding, advice, and constant encouragement in the preparation of the manuscript. I wish to express my appreciation and thanks to Mrs. Martha Smith for her editorial assistance and to Mrs. Kenneth Pease and Miss Brenda Sens for the typing of the manuscript.

A. H. F.

Cambridge, Massachusetts
January, 1960

CONTENTS

MAP

BUARIJ
PORTRAIT OF A LEBANESE MUSLIM VILLAGE

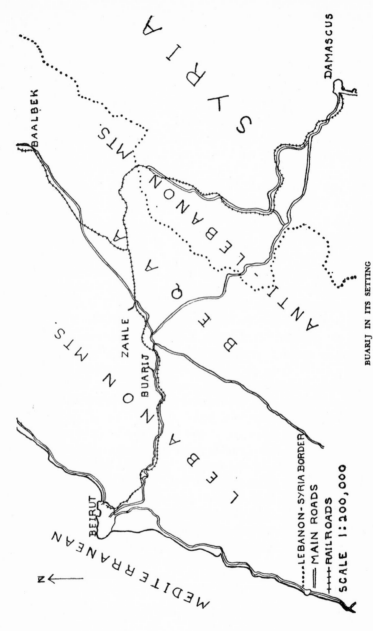

BUARIJ IN ITS SETTING

········· LEBANON-SYRIA BORDER
━━━━━━ MAIN ROADS
+++++ RAILROADS
SCALE 1:200,000

I

THE VILLAGE WORLD

Water is a source of life., Where springs break from the Lebanese mountains there is human habitation. Water is a source of power, feeding and nourishing the soil. Sprites and spirits inhabit sources of water since living water issuing from the hidden regions of the earth is both mysterious and semi-sacrosanct; mysterious because of its subterranean origins, semi-sacrosanct because of its primal relationship to the sustaining of all life.

On the eastern slopes of the Lebanon mountains, which run parallel to the Mediterranean Sea and form a distinguishing mark of the country, from the steep slopes of Mt. Knisseh at an altitude of four thousand feet, breaks a spring of water, *neba asal,* or "spring of honey," so called because of the sweetness and freshness of its flow. Lesser springs lie near it. Close to the waters is an Arab Muslim village, its nearer fields and stand of poplars fed by diverted streams. Here high on the eastern mountain slope, facing the interior of the country, a peasant people have their home and gain a living from the soil.

The spring waters flow downward to the plain, a thousand feet below, or to that elevated tableland, the Beqaa, which divides the Lebanon mountains from the more easterly and parallel Anti-Lebanon range. It is this stretch of territory of downward mountain slope, of width of plain, and face of further mountain range that village houses overlook. The village itself is the highest settlement on the mountain side. It forms the apex of a watered triangle which becomes more populated as the foothills and region of the plain are reached. Within this immediate region the village is a relatively isolated community removed from and set above the more densely populated area of the lower altitudes.

This elevated spot, with its source of water derived from still higher mountain slopes which rise to elevations of seven thousand feet and are snow-capped in winter, must have been long, if intermittently, inhabited, not only because of the life-sustaining springs, but because of the site's strategic outlook commanding a view of the major routes of communication. A Roman sarcophagus, according to village tradition, is said to have been found near the spring. But since the peasants attribute the word "Roman" loosely and to much that pertains to the past, and since the peasant time-sense endows events which have taken place before village history with an exaggerated aura, it is more likely that this so-called sarcophagus was a watering trough of far more recent origin. Nonetheless, ruins of a larger and more extensive town are strewn over village lands.

The village site overlooks the main west-east communications crossing the plain below, linking the Lebanon with the Anti-Lebanon range and ultimately joining the Mediterranean coastal city of Beirut with the Syrian capital of Damascus, a distance of eighty miles. It also overlooks segments of the north-south route following the length of the plain and linking the interior towns of both Lebanon and Syria. The village, as well, is located less than a mile's distance from the mountain pass by which the west-east Beirut-Damascus route descends the eastern slope of the Lebanon range to the plain below. The tarmac Beirut-Damascus highway and a narrow gauge railway, which follow the mountain defile, were both built in the latter part of the nineteenth century.

A caravan route preceded these, while the pass itself has been used as a means of communication across the range from the Mediterranean seacoast to the interior throughout long history, although not until 1858 was a wheeled vehicle used upon the route. The strategic value of the village site with its far-reaching view and proximity to the pass has deteriorated with the growth of the powers of the state. All the same, it has bearing on the history of the village.

Buarij, the name of the village, relates to the former strategic value of the village location. According to one village tradition the name Buarij is derived from *burg*, signifying a "tower" or "turret," the site at an earlier date said to have been utilized as a watch-post for caravans passing over the range. Other village tradition relates that the name Buarij is a corruption of *abu rishi* or "father of feathers." This legendary, or semi-legendary, figure acted as a watchman and, as a semi-autonomous figure, exacted tolls on all caravans passing over the mountain route. By this means he became a man of wealth, sleeping on a bed of feathers.

The present-day inhabitants of Buarij trace the history of their own settlement back to the 1830's. These were disturbed times when Ibrahim Pasha of Egypt invaded the country and is said to have destroyed the former settlement whose foundation stones are found among the vineyards. The ancestors of the present community, dislocated from former sites by the Egyptian invasion, were founders of the present settlement.

The peasants of Buarij consider their village a world of its own. Few persons from the outside world visit or pass through the settlement since it lies at the end of a blind road leading off the Beirut-Damascus highway. Only the occasional visitor enters Buarij, even from the neighboring foothill settlements, since the climb up the steep mountain slope is too arduous for purposes other than business.

Of the several villages within the watered triangle and general area, Buarij is the most isolated. It is isolated by reason of its high mountain position and its location at the end of a blind road. It is also isolated by economic, social, and religious differences which tend to cut it off and distinguish it from its neighbors.

Buarij is the smallest of the communities within the immediate region and numbers no more than 235 persons. It is a poor village, its rocky limestone mountain soil less fertile than that of the foothill communities where several streams collect. It is, moreover, a Muslim community, while neighboring communities are either Christian or of mixed Christian and Muslim population. These foothill communities, furthermore, or those lying on the plain's edge, five in number and situated from a half hour's to more than an hour's walk from Buarij, lie directly on or close to the busy west-east highway and parallel railway track, or on intersecting north-south communications. These settlements, in contrast to the more remote mountain village of Buarij, are in more immediate contact with the larger world and are more exposed to the cross-currents of traffic and its attendant influences. A combination of factors, all of which tend to turn the mountain village in upon itself, therefore serves to differentiate Buarij from neighboring communities.

Yet in considering their village as a world apart, it is not primarily because of the foregoing physical, and other, factors that the inhabitants of Buarij conceive of their village as a separate entity — as do all Lebanese villages in varying degrees — but for more intimate and immediate reasons, all heavily laden with emotional attributes. First, the feeling stems in part from the fact that the village inhabitants are the possessors, utilizers, and inheritors of village land; land which is their own possession and guarantees some means of sustenance. Second, the feeling stems from the close inter-network of blood and marriage ties whereby all persons of the village are related to one another by blood or marriage, or a combination of the two. These ties knit persons into a fabric of mutual obligations, one towards another, enhancing the sense of personal and village security, and marking the community off from the larger world. The village society, patrilineal and patri-local as in other Lebanese communities, counts its descent from the first male ancestors who came to the mountain site. From these five male ancestors and village founders stem the five village clans. Lineage related to inheritance of village land and inter-relation of lineages through intra-clan marriages strengthens the sense of village separateness and village cohesion. The single Sunni Muslim faith is a further mark of common identity.

This trinity of land, kin, and religious ties dominates and shapes the pattern of village life. The interlocking of land, kin, and religious sentiments is strengthened in turn by a common stock of village tradition and lore. Life in other Lebanese villages is also based on the same general sentiments stemming from local, kin, and religious ties, although the outward expression varies in form and intensity in accordance with religious adherence, economic activities, and village location. Back of this body of sentiments which shapes village life itself is the larger geographical and historical picture, which also has bearing on the pattern of village life, although it is not apparent to the villagers themselves, nor does it have the same immediate emotional significance.

The physical terrain of Lebanon, particularly its mountain ranges, splintered by ravines and gorges, combined with the fall of winter snows in the higher altitudes, has served to isolate community from community. The growth of communications, moreover, has been relatively slow. For the country as a whole these were not well established until the first quarter of the twentieth century. Domination by foreign powers — the Ottoman Empire and the French Mandate, following the close of the First World War — has thwarted a sense of national unity, while a general lack of security has added to the sense of the village as a separate world. The religious differentiations which have existed for centuries within the country (the present population being divided into approximately half Muslim and half Christian groups, each subdivided into a variety of sects) have in turn intensified the sense of community parochialism. Religious sects, both Muslim and Christian, moreover, have utilized the rugged mountain territory as a safe refuge from persecution, thereby further enhancing the sense of religious and community isolation. This general geographical, historical, and religious background has bearing on all Lebanese communities.

The plan and structure of the village of Buarij reveal the sense of the village as a separate entity. The plan and structure likewise reveal the close allegiance of the villagers to their immediate physical surroundings. The village fountain, the source of village life, situated to one side of the single dirt road that bisects the village, forms the center of the village community. No household lies more than a ten-minute walk from this flow of water upon which all households depend. The houses, rectangular in shape, flat-roofed, and of one story or two stories stepped back against the mountain side, are built of mud brick and stone, both derived from immediate surroundings. The flat earth roof tops are underlaid by poplar poles cut from village groves. The household frontages and doorways face the downward eastern slope, not only to catch the morning sun, but in order to observe and keep guard over the stretch of village cultivated lands.

All village houses are set in close proximity to one another as a means of unified defense against the outer world and also to ensure all village persons having easy access to one another. There are no outlying buildings except for the brush shelters erected in the fields during the summer season for the guarding of crops. The spatial distribution of houses falls roughly into clan quarters, joint family groups within a clan tending to live next door to each other or to share a composite house, each family possessing its own separate entry door and room, or rooms. This general distribution of houses according to blood bonds reveals the close tie between clan members, including its lesser segmentations, linked to one another by bonds of reciprocal obligations and mutual interdependence. Other than the single store with its attached coffeehouse, a link with the outer world, — situated next to the fountain — the only outstanding building is the village mosque with its outer court and stone tower.

The village structure still further reveals village interests and the dependence on land and livestock. Barnyards walled with stone or thorn bush lie directly before village houses so that animals may be kept under close guardianship. The single sheep or more, the goats, the household donkey, the single cow or brace of oxen are stabled in quarters situated beneath the household living space, their body warmth serving to heat family quarters in winter. The animal manure dropped in household yards serves as dung cakes for household fuel. Within the houses and set against the walls are the clay bins and jars in which produce from the fields and orchards is stored. Dispersed between groups of houses are the several semi-subterranean ovens in which bread is baked. These, for the most part, are clan-owned.

Surrounding the village nucleus are the village lands. Close to the village, so that they may be easily guarded, lie the circular threshing floors, set on flat surfaces open to play of winds. The threshing floors, like the ovens, tend to be clan property. Interspersed between the houses, or close to them, lie the mixed vegetable plots and lesser orchards. These are fed by waters diverted from the spring's overflow, each clan having traditional water rights. The proximity of the garden plots to the houses permits each household to keep a watchful eye over the ripening melons and other produce, and allows as well all persons of a household, old and young, to share in the care of them. Further afield lie the larger orchards of apple, pear, and fig. Situated on the downward slope of the mountain are the more extensive fields of barley and of wheat. Surrounding the village and rising in back of it, stretch the terraced vineyards. These garden plots, orchards, fields, and vineyards are the property of village family groups, or individuals within families, their holdings scattered in a number of dispersed plots over the mountain side. The higher stretch of uncultivable territory, reaching far above the sources of water up to the limestone crags of the mountain height, is grazing and fuel-gathering ground. This is communal village property. The garden plots are watered by irrigation trenches derived from the spring's source, each clan jealously maintaining its traditional water rights. Fields are left fallow for a year or more or crops are rotated in order to renew the vigor of the soil. Following the grain harvest, flocks are pastured for both day and night on the stubble, their droppings fertilizing the ground. The terracing of land both extends the cultivable area and preserves the soil from the run-off of valued rainfall.

Village landholdings, however, do not suffice village needs, though they guarantee to the peasant at all times a minimum of security and the sense of possessing a means of life which is peculiarly his own. Village men augment incomes from village lands by work as sharecroppers on the richer plain lands below. Men also leave home in the slack of the agricultural season, finding work on roads or in the larger towns as unskilled labor, or they obtain work as farm hands in the Mediterranean coastal strip where the agricultural calendar extends throughout the year. This pattern of the seasonal dispersal of labor is common to most of Lebanon and has long been in duration. Three village oldsters even tried their luck as migrants to South America previous to the outbreak of the First World War. The village orbit thus overlaps and intersects with the larger world.

The village is also dependent on the outer world for such food staples as sugar, salt, tea, coffee, olives, and olive oil, as well as for items of clothing, various household utensils, and farm tools. It is likewise linked to the outer world through the tax system, through male participation in district elections, through the district demand for the recording of births, marriages, and deaths, and through the demands for the maintenance of general civil law. Among its inhabitants are wives, brought into the village from elsewhere, and the village *shaykh* and the schoolteacher, both imports from the outer world.

Nonetheless, the villagers conceive of their community as a distinct and separate entity. All village members know its boundaries. All have a strong sense of village loyalty to each other and to the village as a whole. To the outsider, the peasants of Buarij brag of their village waters which are purer than those of the more populated plain's edge where streams grow sullied. They brag of the commanding view from village doorways, stressing its superior outlook in comparison to that of neighboring and less elevated settlements. They brag of themselves, saying that the high mountain air and the rigors of winter give them superior strength. In contrast, they tend to overlook the shortcomings of both themselves and their own village.

Peasant attachment to the village is closely linked to the sense of security the community affords. Here within the village all persons are known to one another, meeting daily on the village paths, at the store, or at the fountain. A similar close knowledge of persons is not shared with the outer world. From close kinsmen in particular each villager may expect help, especially in times of crisis. The world beyond the village orbit does not possess these close ties of blood. Here, land is owned or land will be inherited, which at all times affords a measure of sustenance. The outer world does not possess a similar guarantee of security since the peasant has no tangible stake in it. Within the village is a familiar world of objects and traditions. The outer world does not possess this familiarity. The village is also a world of persons possessing a single faith, all recognizing the oneness and ultimate rule of God.

II

THE WORLD OF TIME AND SPACE

Time to the peasants of Buarij is conceived in qualitative and personal terms rather than in quantitative and abstract terms. Time is thought of not so much in fine-drawn lineal dimensions as in a vague conglomerate of which outstanding events are a part and of its essence, while the notion of time in itself as an isolated abstract entity has little significance. Since time is not conceived of primarily as lineal, entailing a notion of progress or change, the peasants in their general attitude towards life possess a peculiar patience or capacity to wait, believing that things will be revealed within the body of time, since events characterize and are part of time rather than that events can be forced through human endeavor. Certain periods of time or certain days are considered to be auspicious or unauspicious for the undertaking of or abstinence from specific events, or for personal welfare. Accordingly the character of time or its segments is conceived of as bearing influence on man, rather than he giving to it its pattern.

Past time in the peasants' minds fades off beyond the boundaries of their own memories. For three or four generations back, events are kept in fair chronological order. As time recedes, passing beyond the founding of the village, it tends to fall into the general category of "long ago," while the far past takes on the aspect of a golden age interpreted in terms of persons. It is the time of King Solomon and Alexander the Great, both outstanding heroes in Arab lore. These two figures are placed in the same general chronological epoch. Among the peasants it is not so much the quantitative divisions of time that are of significance as its qualitative and emotionally impregnated character. Towards the use of numbers the peasants have a similar qualitative and emotional, rather than a quantitative and analytical, approach. Figures in regard to persons, possessions, and cash are loosely used, except when accuracy benefits the peasant, conveying primarily an emotional reaction rather than any degree of exactitude. Accurate count, moreover, is connected with the demands of the tax collector, an unpopular intruder from the outside world.

The current passage of time among the villagers tends to be defined in terms of the objective world of persons, nature, and local events, which set a rhythm to village activity. Seasons are referred to more often than months in setting a date for outstanding festivals of the Muslim religious calendar or for specific village activities that have a definite time of occurrence, such as the grape harvest. The Christian calendar as well as the Muslim is recognized, its major feast days likewise establishing points of reference, since the peasants in their dealings with the outer world are inevitably brought in contact with Christians. If designating months, the peasants rely on the Christian calendar rather than the Muslim, since the Christian solar count coincides with the seasons or with the basic and visible rhythm of the peasants' agricultural life, while the Muslim calendar in contrast, based upon a lunar count, annually falls eleven days behind the solar year. The Christian calendar, moreover, is the recognized official calendar for business transactions, particularly in dealings with the outer world, its use promoted through French mandate control and through Christian predominance in larger business affairs.

Among the peasants, the age of a child is seldom given in years but is said to be similar to that of a kinsman or neighboring child. The day is rarely broken into the abstraction of numerical hours, but its divisions are designated in terms of the passage of the sun or the moving of shadows thrown by the mountains on the plain below. Or the call to prayer from the village mosque is used as a mark of temporal reference. Watches and clocks are possessed by only a few households and are primarily a symbol of the owner having been to the city. They are regarded more as an ornament similar to a ring or piece of household adornment than as a mechanical means of designating time. When used, they are most often handled in the traditional Muslim and Byzantine manner — each evening reset at the point of twelve to coincide with the moment of sundown, time being conceived of as related to natural order and natural phenomena rather than as a numerical abstraction.

Space likewise is conceived of largely in organic and personal terms rather than in numerical abstractions, and receives most clear-cut definition within the rimmed world with which the peasants have visual and firsthand personal experience. As firsthand familiarity with the spatial world fades off, so in direct ratio does any exactitude of measurable spatial concepts. Spatial measurements, furthermore, are largely given in terms of human activity entailing time duration, although the official metric system is known and referred to by those persons most familiar with the outer world and its marked routes and highways.

The spatial world with which the peasants are most familiar is that rimmed world which they view from village slopes. Within this rimmed world of space, outstanding past temporal events are given fixed location. Noah's Ark is said to have landed on top of Mt. Knisseh on whose slope the village lies. King Solomon is said to have built the Roman temples of Baalbek situated to the north upon the plain. At the foot of Mt. Hermon across the plain lies a buried treasure of Alexander the Great. Thus the era of the golden past is drawn closer at hand by fixing it within known spatial surroundings.

This fusion of past temporal events with known spatial dimensions tends to reinforce lore by localizing it. It gives the past a living background, so making it the more vivid. It brings the past closer to daily experience, for as the peasant feels more at home within his own community, so he feels closer to past temporal events if given spatial setting within the orbit of his own visible horizon. By drawing the noose tighter about time and space the peasant himself secures a firmer place within the flux of events. Like the boundaries of his own village which give him security he also finds boundaries to space and time. The very fact that it is difficult to conceive of space and time apart from village existence and tradition acts, moreover, as a cohesive factor relating the peasant more closely to his environment and establishing the community as a center of gravity. To the peasant the village is the measure of life. Although a small military airport lies upon the plain below the village and although aircraft can be seen making their descents or ascents, no villager has visited the air base, a two-and-a-half hour walk from the mountain home, since curiosity is seldom evinced towards matters that bear no relation to village ways.

The peasant's notions of time and space, personal rather than abstract, qualitative rather than quantitative, and the habit of locating outstanding temporal events in familiar settings bear relation to similar temporal and spatial concepts common to the ancient Near East. And it would appear that this way of conceiving of time and space is a strand from a remoter period of thought which has persisted through the centuries and still persists among the peasant population.*

Yet the peasants of Buarij, despite a habit of personalizing time and space concepts, are not without a knowledge of the larger world and its occurrences. There is the shadowy mysterious story of the sinking of the Titanic and the mountain of ice. There is the tragedy of the Czar of the Muscovites and his innocent children. There is political knowledge drawn from the personal experience of soldiering. There is the current knowledge of political events in Beirut and Damascus and a general sense of the main trend of events in neighboring countries, although these tend to be reported and viewed chiefly in terms of leading per-

---

*For so Pedersen has pointed out the qualitative rather than the quantitative aspects of time among the ancient Hebrews, where "time is charged with substance . . .; time is the development of the very events." (Johannes Pedersen, *Israel, its Life and Culture* I-II [London, 1926], p. 487.) Frankfort, in referring to concepts of space in the ancient Near East, has observed that ". . . primitive thought cannot abstract a concept 'space' from its experience of space." (Henri Frankfort *et al.*, *Before Philosophy, the Intellectual Adventure of Ancient Man* [Penguin ed.; London, 1949], p. 30.) The mythopoeic mode of mind permeating early Near East thought still lingers among the villagers and in terms of primary orientations towards the surrounding world.

sonalities. There is an interest in district elections in which the adult men participate. Here again the interest is in personalities rather than in broader issues. There is the local district paper that comes to the village store. There are the moving pictures witnessed by the men in the larger towns. There are the radios in town coffeehouses.

Yet despite this broader horizon, traditional and local lore continues to lie at the roots of peasant life and plays the more intimate role, giving shape to and preserving the village pattern. Because much of this tradition is localized in a time-space configuration, it is the better ingested and kept alive, while other events in contrast tend to be ephemeral or less concrete in character.

About one-third of the adult village men are literate. But since the accomplishment is not commonly utilized it often falls into atrophy. Only one adult woman can read. She has been lame since early womanhood and her resort to literacy, a late accomplishment, is in part a compensation for her handicap. Village children of the present generation presumably attend the village school up until adolescence. Instruction is extremely rudimentary and attendance irregular. The few girls who attend drop out within a year or two since forms of formal education are not considered to benefit a woman's life. The schoolhouse is a simple one-room building, its wooden benches and sloping ink-stained desks signifying the preoccupation with letters; for according to the villagers every occupation has its proper tools, the two intimately related.

Reading matter, despite the presence of a local newspaper and simple school texts, with short paragraphs on Edison and Lindbergh, remains primarily traditional and sacred. Although school children learn that "the world is round like an apple," chanting it in unison from their school texts, it is the Koran and its context that remains the book of books. Folk tales and legends of early Arab heroes are also popular. A literate member of the community may read aloud to village members on a winter's evening; or the holy writ and hero tales are recited from memory. There is also the common body of village lore handed down orally from one generation to another — the story of the cruel winter when wolves came down from the mountain heights and invaded the village. This has become exaggerated until it is told that a village hero rode off on a wolf's back throttling it with his own hands. Then there is the tale of the sheep thieves from the outer world. And the recitation of the years of starvation following the First World War, when women weakened by hunger crawled on all fours, searching the slopes for wild greens for their dying children. Lesser stories of sprites and spirits, some encountered by the villagers themselves, are recounted, along with folk sayings, riddles, and the singing or reciting of village or local folk songs and verses. Despite possible means of access to a larger body of literature, the peasants prefer to draw upon that which has been and is part of their local tradition, is most related to their own way of life, and which serves to strengthen and support it. In so doing the peasants' minds are continually nourished by an order that has already been established.

Although the world that lies within village boundaries and which can be viewed from village slopes is that with which the peasants are most familiar, the village inhabitants are not without firsthand knowledge of the world that lies beyond the visible horizon. Older men served in the First World War in various parts of the then Ottoman Empire. There are the few men who spent some years in South America. Aside from the men who as sharecroppers work on the landed estates on the plain below the village, there are those who leave the community in the slack of the agricultural season to find work elsewhere on the coastal plain or in other regions. Village herdsmen, moreover, must take the flocks across the range to the warmer Mediterranean coastal area for winter grazing. All these persons, however, return to the village or are expected to return. A wife with grown children still awaits the return of her husband who went over twenty years ago to Argentina. It is primarily because of economic reasons that men leave home in order to augment family incomes. It is primarily because of sentiment that they return.

This deep-rooted sentiment stems from the feeling that whatever may be the momentary economic advantages of the larger world, ultimate security, not necessarily dominated by economic forces, exists and persists within the village orbit. For here there are always kinsmen and people of one's own blood to whom the peasant may turn. Here is the plot of land enduring through generations. Here is the familiar world which, through lore and tradition, has nourished the peasant since childhood. Here within the village is an emotional form of security not found elsewhere. The village is conceived of as the ultimate place to which the peasant belongs.

Village women have far less experience with the outer world than men. The spatial orbit of their lives is primarily confined to village homes and fields. Occasionally a young girl previous to marriage goes into domestic service for a short time in Beirut. But this is regarded as unfortunate and usually pertains to a widow's daughter. Twice a year or so women may go in groups, or accompanied by their men, to buy necessary household supplies at the town of Zahle, the district center, a three-hours' walk. A small minority have travelled the sixty miles east to Damascus, by bus or train, usually to buy wedding furnishings. Almost all adult women have gone at least once to Beirut, an hour's distance by bus. Certain of the women follow their kinsmen or husbands to the coast for winter grazing. Women, however, never leave the village boundaries unaccompanied, except to the nearest foothill settlements. These missions always involve some necessary task such as obtaining medicine from a foothill pharmacy or transporting grain on donkey back to the foothill water mill for grinding. The missions are never excursions of frivolous pleasure or sightseeing.

Women themselves have little interest in mingling and mixing with the larger world. They complain of headaches from the noise and confusion on return from visits to the towns. They feel ill at ease outside village boundaries, for since childhood a woman has had instilled within her that her place is at home. Here surrounded by kinsmen, especially her father and brother, a woman is sure of protection. In her own community a woman has status and security; outside its boundaries, unaccompanied and alone, she can be certain of neither.

Because women are more closely identified with the spatial and personal boundaries of the community, it is their sex which is the most familiar with the details of village lore and village gossip. It is likewise their sex which is the main repository and transmitter of village tradition and lore. Since women play the greater role in child-rearing it is they who most affect the education of the child, transmitting and impressing upon it a traditional view of life. Women are the conservative factor in the village influencing the over-all tone of the community. It is their sex which tends most to promote the feeling and concept of the village as a world in itself. Since they do not leave the community freely and only rarely accompany their men on the latter's longer sojourns from home, their confinement to the village is in itself a strong influence in drawing men back to the community and in maintaining the village as the permanent focal point.

Men are inevitably affected by their participation in the larger world. Their conversation, in contrast to women's, includes far greater reference to the outer orbit, its political happenings, the general state of the crops, the chances of employment, and news of any unusual event. Yet on return to the village from beyond its borders men easily fall back into the general pattern of village ways. Even the men who have spent several years in South America fall back quickly into the village pattern. With their earnings they may enlarge an orchard or vineyard or build a new house. But their lives in no way appear to be perceptibly altered by their sojourn abroad. Only the watch that no longer runs, a batch of colored postal cards, or an out-dated picture calendar are tangible evidence of their years in foreign parts.

Since childhood, persons have sensed that the village is its own world. Conformity to village ways brings approbation, while without group or kinship approval personal security diminishes. Thus the peasant on returning home falls back into the village picture in order that he may be provided with the forms of security the village affords. Yet it is through men's contact with the larger world that changes in the village most readily accrue. New types of dress or tools are introduced. New ideas sift down. Nevertheless, the weight of tradition tends to stand against sudden or radical change.

Concepts of time and space — and the manner of regarding both in personal rather than in abstract terms — relate to the general outlook of the peasants which is primarily personal. Interest in temporal events, past and present, is selective and personal in accordance with the peasants' body of general knowledge and experience. Excursions into the larger world are of limited influence, since the peasants judge the outer world by the personal standards of their own village. The village itself is a personal world, its tradition and lore handed down orally from one generation to another, with its people, related by blood or marriage or a combination of the two, laying emphasis primarily on the personal ties that link peasant to peasant. Within this known world of persons the peasant feels most at home.

III

THE WORLD OF NATURE

The village of Buarij is set within and surrounded by the world of nature. Mountain slope and stretch of plain rather than man-made objects dominate the landscape, while man's handiwork in itself reflects the close dependence on natural surroundings. The village houses of mud and stone blend and are at one with the earth and rock from which and upon which they are built. Earth, rock, water, and growing things are the handiwork of God. By Him was the natural world created. By Him it is sustained. Towards all nature's forms the peasant has a sense of piety, since they are signs of deity and since they relate closely to his own welfare. Towards these sources of his being, on which his own life depends, the peasant shows reverent attachment. Certain trees are considered holy; their branches are not cut. The grain of wheat bears upon it the single indentation or stroke of the Arabic letter *alif*, the first letter of God's name.

But it is to land — land on which wheat is sown and from which bread comes — that the peasant's emotions in the world of nature are most closely tied. Land was there at the time of man's birth. It will be there after his departure. The endurance of earth is its stabilizing quality. To own a plot of land is to participate in that stability. A village through ownership of land partakes of that stability. A household through ownership of land has a guarantee, though often minimal, of its own life course. It also has assurance for the life of coming generations. From the peasant's viewpoint there is neither community nor family without land or work on land.

Land is a conservative influence. Its contours remain essentially the same from generation to generation. Man in a sense must subordinate himself to it, accepting the play of physical forces which lie outside his control. The conservative and traditional forces of the village are in part related to and derived from close association with land.

Family and kinship sentiments are deeply tied up with land. The amount of land owned is a sign of the family's social and basic economic status. Since land abides and generations pass away, it is the permanent factor in the family-land relationship and a tangible symbol on which the family line is based. A man, moreover, plants not only for himself but for future generations, since orchards may well come to bear after he is part and parcel of the soil.

Land is regarded with piety, with strong emotion involving possessiveness and jealous guardianship, and with a strong sense of the practical in terms of its productive powers, in accordance with the peasant's agricultural knowledge. Neither land nor nature as a whole, however, is considered as an isolated aesthetic spectacle or as a subject of abstract contemplation. Rather, landscape and nature take on an emotional connotation in terms of the peasant's personal relation to them. All village pasture lots, fields, groves, and outstanding landmarks have specific names and are known to all. The sweeping view seen from village thresholds is primarily admired because it belongs peculiarly to the village and is an extension of, and from, village doorways. Potted herbs and flowers about household yards find appreciation because they have become part of the household and are cared for by household hands.

Yet at one and the same time an over-all generalized feeling of man's relationship to nature and his consanguinity with nature exists, feeding the peasant emotionally. Folk songs are filled with metaphors and similes expressed in terms of the natural and flowering world. Proverbs and pithy sayings are likewise expressed in terms of physical surroundings and creature inhabitants.

The seasons control the output of the land. The rhythm of the peasants' lives, based on the soil, is in cadence with that of the seasons. The Lebanese year, in accordance with the general climatic pattern of the eastern Mediterranean area, falls into two major divisions, a wet season and a dry season. In late September the lesser rains begin to fall, with snow covering the higher mountain peaks of the Lebanon range during January and February, the months of heaviest precipitation. By late March the rains dwindle and ebb. The remaining part of the year is bright with sun and practically rainless. The dry season is the time of full congregation of village members within the mountain community. The wet winter season is a period of partial village dispersal.

The dry season is the busiest time in the peasant's year. With the retreat of the snows and the ebbing of the rains, work begins in the vineyards — setting out new vines, tending the soil, and repairing the terraced walls damaged by the heavier rains. Meanwhile, closed wooden shutters and wooden doors of village houses are flung open to the growing warmth of sunlight. The family quarters are aired, the sheep-wool quilts and other household equipment are moved into the sunlight, while household walls, dampened by the winter rains, are freshly coated with a thin wash of mud stiffened with animal dung and then overlaid with a coat of whitewash. This is obtained from the chalky earth of a neighboring mountain flank across the plain to which the villagers make excursions.

With the coming of spring warmth the sheep are sheared, the wool being kept for stuffing of quilts, for spinning by the older women, and for making sweaters and socks. At the same time work on the land continues. Spring plowing and sowing take place. The garden plots are prepared and planted. By mid-May these begin to bear. Throughout the summer season the garden work of weeding, watering, and picking continues.

August is the time of the grain harvest on the mountain side, although it falls some weeks earlier for those of the village men who work as sharecroppers on the less elevated plain. Throughout Lebanon as a whole the agricultural calendar fluctuates in accordance with climatic conditions, which vary from coastal area to mountain region depending on altitude and distance inland from the Mediterranean Sea. During the busy weeks of reaping and threshing all available village hands turn into the fields and on to the threshing floors. This is the period of greatest village activity.

Crops brought from the fields, orchards, and gardens are in large part converted into food stores for winter consumption, the flat roof tops serving as sorting and drying areas. Here grain, lentils, and beans are spread on goat-hair rugs, and sorted and sieved previous to being stored within the clay bins. Figs, tomatoes, and eggplants are sliced open and laid in the heat of the summer sun for drying and preserving purposes. Figs and tomatoes are further converted into pastes by slow simmering in outdoor caldrons over brush and dung fires.

Late August and September is the time of the grape harvest. These are days of merriment since they signify the drawing to a close of the agricultural season. Grapes are converted into winter stores, being dried as raisins on roof tops or made into a thick grape treacle used as a spread on bread. This latter process entails the trampling on grapes with naked feet and the boiling of the fluid over outdoor fires. Only men tread on the grapes, their trousers heightened to their knees, since this is considered an unseemly procedure for women.

Meanwhile throughout the summer months, the fat-tailed sheep are forcibly fed and fattened on mulberry and other leaves, brought continually from the orchards. The animals are kept in the shade and carefully tended, watered, and rinsed, since the over-feeding process is hazardous. The loss of a sheep from careless handling is considered a major disaster, a household thereby losing an important food supply. Towards the end of September falls the sheep-slaughter and the conversion of the fatty meat into valued cooking fat for use throughout the year. The sheep-slaughter and the treading on grapes and their boiling both partake of a social occasion, the more so since the two occupations are held out-of-doors. Households join one another in the work of butchering and treading. Over the village rises the smoke from the fires used in preparing both the sheep's fat and the grape treacle. Persons comment on the agreeable smell of their village, the acrid smoke of the dung fires combining with the heavy smell of meat and the sweet scent of the pressed and simmering grapes. It is a smell that tells of food for the winter.

Late autumn is the time for village ceremonies. Cash is on hand from the sale of excess crops to the outside world. All persons are still collected in the village. Circumcisions, marriage contracts, and weddings most often take place in late autumn during the brief respite after the harvest and before the fall of the heavier rains. These group ceremonies, falling in the autumn, serve to impress upon the peasant his tie to the community and its life-sustaining lands before the partial dispersal of persons for the winter season.

With the coming of the October rains, the winter plowing commences. Vineyards and orchards are pruned, meanwhile. But along with the commencement of the rains and their increase in volume, persons begin to desert the village for the warmer and more populated coastal area on the western side of the Lebanon range. Young unmarried men drift off to find work as unskilled labor either in Beirut and its environs or in the olive and citrus groves of the Mediterranean coastal strip. A plowman having completed the work on his own lands takes the same route, descending to sea level altitudes where agricultural work continues throughout the winter. Shouldering his plow and driving his brace of oxen before him, he takes leave of his family.

Before the first fall of snow the herdsmen depart, escorting the goats to the same lowland area. They take with them all of the village goats, householders paying them for their services in a share of the kids. The flocks are grazed in regions with which the herdsmen have established traditional relations over a period of years, returning each winter to the same site. Other high mountain villages in Lebanon pursue a similar grazing rhythm returning annually to established winter grazing lands. Payment for use of the grounds is in animal manure dropped in the night shelters of caves or enclosures which herdsmen and flocks inhabit together. Women of the family sometimes accompany the herdsmen, a wife with small children departing with her husband; or an old grandmother tags along in order to avoid the rigors of the mountain winter.

Persons away from home for the winter season attempt to find work in the same general neighborhood of one another, feeling at all times the need to associate with those with whom they have

strongest ties. The single plowman after his day's work seeks out
the herdsmen's shelter and shares in their meal. The young unmarried men come on foot or by bus from the suburbs of Beirut
to call on the herdsmen families. As a result, a lesser village community is established even though persons are absent from home,
and the sense of tie with the mountain community is not entirely
disrupted.

Approximately one-fourth of the village is absent from home
during the winter season, some persons leaving for only a few
weeks at a time, others for a number of months. But no mountain
household is ever entirely deserted. Always some members of the
family or close kinsmen remain on the mountain side to keep
guard over the food stores and the family lands, and in order to
remove the damaging weight of snow from the flat roof tops of
the houses. Villagers away from home thus remain linked to one
another not only by establishing a lesser community of individuals
in contact with one another in the lowlands but by still retaining
close personal and property ties in the mountain community.
Men, moreover, return from the lowlands to the mountain home
on intermittent visits, bringing oranges and other coastal foodstuffs or a bit of cash from their earnings. The tie with the mountain community is thus in essence maintained despite the partial
winter dispersal.

Meanwhile, within the village, houses are made safe against the
coming of winter. The poplar rafters are strengthened, and a fresh
layer of earth and gravel is packed and rolled on the roof tops.
Stacks of dung cakes and faggots are piled against doors for use
on the hearths. Food is sealed in bin and jar and stored in niches
along the walls. Strings of onions and garlic hang from the rafters.
The remaining animals are stabled beneath the house, their heat
warming the household quarters. Goat-hair rugs are spread on
the floor, and wooden shutters are sealed with mud against the
coming of winter. Almost all outdoor activity is at a standstill
except for the necessary journeys to the fountain. In event of deep
snow on the mountain pass, however, village men are called out
to clear both the highway and the railway line. This clearing of
the snow, which is a means of earning cash, is considered their

prerogative, since their village, in contrast to those of the foothill area, lies nearest the region of deep snowfall.

Within doors a close community life flourishes. About the hearth stories are read aloud or told, village tradition and lore thereby being rekindled and transmitted. Young girls learn sewing from their mothers, while boys help with the repair of farm tools and harness. Old persons turn to crafts, the men weaving baskets of withes, the women spinning or knitting. Winter is the time when the peasants turn most towards the traditional and are most drawn into themselves. Like animals, they themselves say, they hibernate.

As the snows retreat and the rains ebb, those who have left the village drift home singly or in pairs, the young men with cash in their belts, the herdsmen, with their flocks, anxious to reach the mountain home before the kids are dropped. Cash and free-flowing milk, aside from the returning persons, are eagerly welcomed by the mountain community, beginning to feel the pinch of dwindling food supplies at the end of the winter season.

On the plain the greening of wheat is beginning to show. Green in itself is a holy color connected with all vegetation. On the mountain side persons comment gladly as the fresh growth breaks through the soil. It signifies that spring has returned to the mountain and that life is beginning to return to the land from which stores may be replenished. With the greening of ground, the great spring festival falls. Peasants hasten back to the mountain to take part in this greatest of annual events, which celebrates both the return of people to the homes to which they belong and the return of life to the land. The springtime festival, as will be seen later, also serves to impress upon the peasant man's dependence on the world of nature, wherein acknowledgment is made of the creative and sustaining power of God in whose hands lies the rhythm of all life, its seasons and its constant regeneration.

IV

THE WORLD OF PEOPLE

The peasants of Buarij are primarily interested in themselves and in their own village. Yet back of their own lives and all life is always the image of God upon whom all creation depends. Because God is the giver of life, all life is holy.

The villagers accordingly consider it wrong to willfully interfere with the life process either in the foetal stage or during the life course. Yet women do at times induce miscarriage, although in secrecy and with fear of discovery and attendant condemnation. When abortion is resorted to, it is usually to preserve life already on hand and because the household means of sustenance cannot easily support another additional member. Birth control through use of any form of artificial contraceptive is considered interference with divine will. No suicide is known to have taken place in the village.

The mentally aberrated or mentally retarded are considered to be possessed by powers beyond their control, combining both the demonic and the holy. Towards such persons there is an ambivalent attitude of fear mixed with reverence. Unbalanced persons in the neighborhood are often spoken of. To some, especially epileptics, is attributed the gift of prophecy. Such persons play a role in festivals, the crowds gathering about them.

In the peasants' mind, back of all life lies the image of God. Beyond all life is again God's image. To the villagers, the years of man's life, coming from God and returning to God, are a span wherein terrestrial knowledge accrues through experience. The small child, though admonished, is forgiven his misdemeanors since it is said he has not yet gained understanding. In contrast, the old by reason of their accumulation of years and their wide participation in village life are said to know — to have understanding. The old are accordingly held in respect and their council is sought in household and village decisions. The old, since their life course is ebbing, are considered near God, whose knowledge is beyond the sum total of all men's knowledge. Thus the old not only partake of the sum of terrestrial knowledge, but also, because of their proximity to death, approach that greater knowledge which pertains to deity. Old persons, both men and women, take to individual prayer and fasting, realizing that the hand of the Creator is closing upon them.

Adult men and women, as well as adolescents, are expected to conduct themselves within the accepted pattern of village behavior. The habit of ostracizing the non-conformist and cutting him off from participation within the household or village group tends to hold or bring the individual into line, especially since the individual is aware that the greatest assurance of personal security depends on the maintenance of village ties. This awareness in itself acts as a deterrent from aberrant action.

Formal village government is in the hands of the village *mukhtar* or "chief," and the council of male elders, both elected to their positions by all adult heads of village households. Serious breaches of custom and law are committed to their judgment. Punishment is usually in the form of material restitution by the offender to the injured party or parties. The village chief and council of elders make a strong effort to avoid taking disputes before persons of the outer world or to the district court. This is airing of village linen in public and tends to injure the village name and reputation in surrounding communities. Besides, the village considers itself a world apart, concerned with and capable of managing its own personal affairs.

Within the village there is great conformity in thought and behavior. All persons share more or less in the same body of knowledge reinforced by the same traditions. All persons, aside from age and sex differences, perform the same general tasks or are familiar with them. All persons, moreover, live in close contact with one another, families within a single room, joint family groups under the same roof or close at hand. This close household and village living tends to blur the lines between individuals and inhibits the growth of individualism. It is the family or joint family, furthermore, that is the economic unit, not the individual. Since the primary need of life is sustenance, the individual cannot easily break with the larger food-producing unit.

There is an extraordinary lack of privacy of any kind within the village. This lack of privacy in itself curbs individual growth and behavior. All household comings and goings can be viewed by next-door neighbors. Individual action falls under the eyes of other members of the household. All village persons meet daily on the paths or at the fountain or store. In this tight-knit world of persons it is thought wrong to seek out solitude. Nor do the villagers appear to desire it. The ill and ailing are visited by a host of relatives and friends, and these visits are expected. A woman in childbirth is surrounded by neighboring women, often accompanied by their smaller children. Apart from the group the individual's life loses meaning. Within the group it is fortified and strengthened by the presence of others.

Although the growth of individualism is curbed, the possession of specific personal traits and characteristics is recognized. There is the village wit and the village dullard, the morose woman and her hearty sister, the man with authority and the man who is a weakling. Persons are often bantered or given nicknames in accordance with their personal traits. But these characteristics should not be such as to disrupt village ways. For the independent-minded man, however, there remains an avenue of escape from village conformity. This is to prolong his sojourns outside of the village. The strong-minded man, particularly if still unmarried, may resort to spending extended periods of time outside the mountain community. If he returns bringing cash to the household, his prolonged absence is forgiven. A long-term absence, however, may well result in other persons of a household taking over his share of the land and by right of usufruct refusing to return it. Punishment of the troublemaker by village government in extreme cases may entail temporary banishment from the community, or even total exile.

There are no class differences within the village, although some families possess more wealth than others through larger landholdings or more lucrative work outside the village. This differentiation does not create marked social differences since all household are engaged in the same basic enterprises and all are attached to the soil. There is a feeling of jealousy, however, towards persons who possess more, for the villagers live so close to the margin of bare existence that envy of others in terms of income is easily aroused. The degree of comparative wealth of various households is a constant subject of conversation. A tendency exists to look down on, or at least to regard as less fortunate, those few families who because of small landholdings make their living primarily from goat-herding.

There is no real full-time specialization of labor in the community except for the *shaykh* and the schoolteacher, both imports from the outside world. The so-called village cobbler combines his skill with the tending of his lands and is averse to mending footwear if and when it interferes with his main agricultural pursuits. The so-called village barber may or may not condescend to cut hair at the end of the day after his return from the fields, depending on his own mood and needs. The storekeeper in a sense is a specialist but is not so recognized in village eyes, since it is believed that any man could perform his duties just as well. He, too, combines storekeeping with care of his lands. The village seamstress is the nearest person to a specialist, but since she has been lame for years and is also a widow, her single occupation is recognized as a necessary economic adjustment. Specialization of labor is frowned upon, since it tends to identify a peasant with a town way of life or a way of life that is not specifically his own. It is to the towns that peasants expect to go for specialized services of one kind or another. That is what towns are for.

Although there is no real specialization of labor in the community, persons vary in their ability to perform tasks. This variation is recognized, as are personal traits and characteristics, and utilized by all members of the community. It is expected of the skilled individual that he will contribute his talents to help others, and not necessarily for recompense. The woman with most skill at midwifery is expected to be present at a childbirth. The man most skilled at butchery automatically goes from house to house at the time of the sheep-slaughter. These persons, furthermore, take a certain pride in their skill and expect it to be utilized by others, while their personal prestige within the community is enhanced through their contributions.

Peasant aversion to full specialization of labor stems not only from the feeling that specialization belongs to the towns and is therefore not a true mark of peasant life but because specialization cuts the individual off from the group, differentiating him from others. It builds a partial man unable to participate in the whole life of the community. In contrast, through knowledge of all tasks common to the community, one person may the more readily replace the other either within the economic kin unit or within village activity as a whole. By all persons having approximate knowledge of the same tasks, greater harmony of interests and efforts is achieved, village friction is thereby reduced and greater personal unity attained. An individual, moreover, as a member and extension of his kin line is expected to represent not only his blood lineage but the activities with which his family is, and has been, identified. Specialization of labor is frowned upon because it departs from the established and traditional. In Lebanese Christian villages, in contrast to Muslim villages, there is less emphasis on close kinship ties, particularly in terms of close kin marriage which is forbidden in the nearer degrees. Accordingly, there is less stress on adherence to family traditional occupations; Christians, in contrast to Muslims, thereby break more readily from established modes of occupation and more freely alter the pattern of their lives.

The village sense of persons equating one another and all being theoretically equipped to participate in the same activities invades the concept of village government. The village chieftainship theoretically rotates from one clan to another, but if the existing chief is a particularly impressive personality and is further fortified by landholdings larger than those of the majority of households, his tenure of office may well be prolonged. Because of his character and comparative wealth, he is able to make a strong impression both within the village and in village dealings with the outer world. The council of elders is represented by members from each clan. The coveted job of watchman of village lands theoretically passes annually from clan to clan and is paid for by a portion of each householder's crops. Here, again, if the watchman is an especially strong character, whose bearing impresses both the villagers and the outside world, he may well retain his office for longer than an annual term. By rotation of village offices, no clan comes into too great power, nor does any one person assume a fixed role. In village life, village equilibrium is the end in view. From the peasant's viewpoint, this is best attained when village activities, persons, households, and clans most approximately equate one another. When concessions are made to this outlook, it is primarily in order to gain greater village solidarity or more strength in facing the outside world.

The *shaykh* and the schoolteacher, both imported from the outside world, are not regarded as true village members. Neither has kinship ties within the community. Neither has land, although the *shaykh,* who is married but childless, has been let a plot of land for whose rent and cultivation he pays in a share of the crop. The *shaykh's* services are paid for by a Beirut Muslim philanthropic organization; the schoolteacher is provided by the state. The villagers, however, make small token gifts in cash or crops for any special services rendered. Towards the *shaykh* a certain respect is shown because of his religious position and knowledge of holy writ. The best, and often only, chair is accorded him if he visits a home, and coffee is immediately proffered. The schoolteacher, on the other hand, a recent innovation, is not taken with great seriousness but is regarded as an intrusion from the outside world, whom the village of necessity must tolerate. He, in contrast to the *shaykh,* squats on his heels or sits on a low stool when making a visit, and may or may not receive coffee according to the dictates of his host. Although neither the *shaykh* nor the schoolteacher is treated with the familiarity that one villager accords another and much of the village gossip is kept from their ears, there is an attitude of tolerance towards both. This tolerance is even mixed with a feeling of compassion as if both persons deserved a modicum of pity, since they have been uprooted from the place of their origin and neither has close-at-hand family ties. As outsiders, they both lack, from the peasant's viewpoint, the essential ingredients for a stable and meaningful existence. The young bachelor schoolteacher, moreover, is regarded with some suspicion lest, lonely and unmarried, he make advances to village girls.

In the close-knit village world where all persons are linked to one another through bonds of blood and marriage and through the sense of individuals equating one another, the sentiment of loyalty involving mutual obligations dominates all others. First, there is loyalty to the family or joint family. Next, there is loyalty to the clan. At one and the same time allegiance to the community is exhibited, all village members rallying as one and forgetting other rivalries if faced by a threat from the outer world. Assault or insult of a village member by a non-village member and destruction or theft of village property by an outsider immediately arouse the whole village. On such occasions men rally at the store and coffeehouse, while women congregate in groups. The first reaction is for the village to take the law into its own hands, to march on an offending village, or to assault the offender and his kinsmen. But the growth of state law inhibits the first feeling of village retaliation. The local gendarme, who makes his routine visit on horseback, is resorted to, or the case is brought before district courts. In describing the offense to representatives of the outer world, the villagers have little or no compunction in adhering to objective facts. False witnesses are presented or the story is highly colored in favor of the village's point of view. Truth, as the villagers say, is what is felt in the heart, and the heart feels allegiance to the village home first and foremost.

Punishment of the villagers by authorities of the outside world for trespass on, and damage of, other villagers' lands, for assault on an outsider, or for evasion of taxes is considered a misfortune, but not a disgrace, by the village inhabitants. Many a village man has spent a short term in the district jail, to be feasted and welcomed by the community on his return. Nor are the laws and regulations of the outer world taken with any great seriousness unless they happen to be of use to the peasants' position. Men hold firearms illegally for they consider that each house has the inborn right to self-protection. Cheating the tax collector is accepted as laudable behavior.

Among persons of the outside world, the villagers feel most at ease with those who most nearly equate themselves. The mark of common faith, combined with the possession of a common body of customs and traditions, is an accepted mark of common allegiance. Religion in Lebanon, moreover, with its two major divisions of Muslims and Christians and with a diversity of lesser sects, is the center about which persons automatically adhere, especially in times of crisis. The peasants tolerate other peasants more readily than they do city dwellers or desert nomads, whose ways of life differ radically from their own. They tolerate and accept persons from their own general neighborhood more readily than persons from beyond the spatial horizon of their own world. In all relationships with the outer world, the villagers take their own community as point and standard of reference. To the peasants of Buarij, their own village is the measure of all things.

V

THE WORLD OF CHILDREN

Married couples expect and look forward to having children, for all living creatures produce their kind. It is a law of life as ordained by God the Creator. Through sons, the patrilineal line is secured and projected into unborn generations. Through children, especially sons, care and upkeep of the family lands are assured. Children are insurance against the exigencies of old age for they help provide for their aging parents. Moreover, a village to survive and face the outer world must have numbers.

Sweets are handed out to visitors at the birth of a male child. This may or may not be done at the birth of a daughter. Throughout life, the male offspring possesses more prerogatives than the female, since in Muslim society it is the male who is regarded as the more elevated of the two sexes among the creatures of God.

The newborn child severed from the umbilical cord enters into a world with which it is unfamiliar and to which it is a stranger. Like any stranger in a new community or like the peasant himself in the outer world, the infant is exposed to the unknown and is unknown. To these hazards is added the additional risk of its own physical frailty. The small infant in its precarious position is thus vulnerable to the malicious influence of the *jinn* or "evil spirits." In order to protect the child the placenta is buried before the doorstep, while the first soiled diapers are placed in the air vent above the door. Accordingly, the interior of the house, the child's first terrestrial home, is made safe. To the baby's bonnet or dress a blue bead is attached to ward off the evil eye, or a phylactery bearing holy writ may be strung around its neck. The child may wear these and other charms for some years.

The small infant is kept tightly swaddled. The binding, it is said, protects its fragility, particularly when the baby is handed from one person to another. The first four or five months the infant spends largely in the cradle or in the arms and lap of its mother and grandmother, although even small children may fondle and take the baby about. No serious attempt is made to toilet train the child. A hole in the cradle to which a chamber pot is attached acts as a receptacle for excretions. When a child begins to toddle about, it goes without panties, uses the family hearth and its bed of ashes, or is mopped up after much like an un-housetrained puppy. There is little or no feeling of filth connected with a child's excretions, especially during the nursing period. Even the adults use the outdoors indiscriminately for their own excretions, and those few families who possess outhouses do not use them with any regularity.

The child is breast-fed for about a year, although this may be extended to two or more years. It is taken to the breast whenever it shows discontent or hunger. Small toddlers, still breast-fed, come running and searching for their mothers' breasts as they please. Prolonged breast-feeding is an accepted method of spacing children. If a child feeds from a wet nurse, which may be necessary because of a mother's illness or inability to give milk or even because of her temporary absence in the fields, the child is considered sibling to the wet nurse's own children, and future marriage between the children related by milk is forbidden. Occasionally, a village girl sighs that she cannot marry such and such a young man since they fed from a common breast. This injunction against marriage of milk kin is in accordance with Koranic law.

The child moves by graduated steps from breast-feeding to the family dish, in which all household members dip their bread. First, the mother may soften a bit of bread or other food in her own mouth before giving it to the child. As soon as a child can use its own hands, it comes to participate more and more in the family meal. By sitting around the common plate, it is introduced to the kin circle, comprised of the immediate family or the family and the paternal grandparents. The common dish is a symbol of the kin food-producing unit and is related in turn to the land, the ultimate source of nourishment.

When a child can stand upright and fend for itself, or when it begins to shed its milk teeth, a small rite may take place wherein a child's hands are dipped in a bowl of flour. The child's upright position and full use of its hands signifies that it now belongs to the family of man. As man it will partake of human economy which is the getting of bread from the soil. Besides, bread is holy. It should neither fall on the ground nor its scraps be tossed aimlessly aside. So the child is introduced into the world of piety and faith, wherein reverence is due to the sources of life which stem from and are of God.

The nursing child is naturally most often with its mother, although it is passed from lap to lap much like a pet or toy. Fathers are not averse to carrying a child through the streets, the men of the village dandling and fondling it. But, next to its mother, it is the grandparents who have most to do with a child. It is their special comfort. Grandmothers often take a small child to bed in their arms to increase their own failing body heat. Young children are left much of the time with their grandparents, paternal or maternal, while the mother and other members of the family are busy in the gardens or fields. Because of the close association of grandchild and grandparent, a conservative and traditional outlook is instilled into the child at a young age, the child's viewpoint being molded by that of a passing generation.

Small brothers and sisters treat each other much as equals and are so treated by their elders, although there is always a predilection to favor the boy. A growing boy, however, soon begins to realize the favored status of his sex and may bully, and make demands on, his sisters accordingly. Pre-adolescent girls in their turn rapidly become aware that the life of their sex is primarily related to care of the home and children. At a young age they begin to share in the care of the younger children, lugging them about on their still childish hips and feeding and dressing them.

Both growing son and daughter show more affection and intimacy towards the mother than the father. Between daughter and mother a close bond develops which extends throughout life. This bond relates to the close ties that exist between members of the same sex in contrast to the social lines of distinction drawn between members of the opposite sex. Son and daughter, as well as mother, tend to treat the father with respect tinged with fear. The choicest morsels of food or the largest share of the plate are set aside for the father who comes in from the fields. Daughter and mother both hasten to wash his feet at the end of the working day, while the growing son will move aside, knowing the most comfortable corner of the house is reserved for the father who takes most care of the lands.

The attitudes learned in the home towards persons in relation to age and sex are extended outward through the community in diminishing degrees of intensity in accordance with age, sex, and kinship ties. Towards paternal grandparents, who may eat from the common dish and so form part of a joint family, an attitude of respectful deference is shown, though the growing child often retains a bond of intimacy with the grandmother who has tended its needs and even spoiled it when young. Paternal uncles are treated much like the father since they stand nearest to him in terms of kinship, both being of the same generation and sprung from the same parents. Towards all paternal kin there is stronger allegiance than towards the maternal kin, in accordance with the patrilineal and patrilocal structure of the community.

Children take the first name of the father as a surname. A first-born male may take his father's surname as a first name. By repetition of this reversing system through three generations, the grandchild's first name and surname in respective order duplicate the first name and surname of the paternal grandfather. Thus alternate paternal generations may be linked through repetition of name, the grandson in name reincarnating the paternal grandfather and so replacing a failing generation, and at one and the same time renewing the family line. The clan name, which follows the first name and surname, is the name of the first male ancestor who came to the village. The clan name is not usually used in common everyday life but is referred to in formal registrations or when more definite designation is needed.

Boys' names in particular are of religious connotation, referring to a figure in Muslim history or based on one of the many similes for the name of God; or they may be descriptive of religious attributes. The name "Mohammed" is the most popular. Names that have definite Christian association are not used, although there is a common stock of names utilized by both faiths. After first name, surname, and clan name, the name of the village may be attached. This is used primarily when the peasant is outside the confines of his village home, designating to the outer world the place from which he comes. The nomenclature system thus places the individual within the context of family, lineage, and locality, and may reflect religious affiliation as well. The system itself is an outward manifestation of the peasant's tie to family and lineage, locality, and religious faith — those three sentiments that dominate and shape his life.

A child's responsibilities, both physical and social, increase gradually in accordance with physical growth and expansion of mind. Children are rarely punished severely, since offenses and misdemeanors are attributed to a child's inexperience with life. Children, however, are bantered and teased by their elders, who find their bewildered reactions entertaining. A child's education is informal rather than formal, although there may be four or five years of intermittent and inferior schooling. A child learns the most through imitation and observation of, and participation in, the activities of his elders and older siblings. A child begins to work scarcely knowing that it is work. He fetches and carries things about the yard as soon as his strength permits. Children of seven or over watch the flocks in the nearer fields, carry food to their fathers at work, and share in the care of the house and nearby garden plots. Girls at a young age begin to imitate their mothers at work at their household tasks. Boys as they grow older begin to leave the yard to accompany the men to the further fields. By the time of adolescence a girl is familiar with all household tasks including the baking of bread. This achievement places her in the separate world of adult women, for bread-making is essentially women's work and the communal oven is considered her domain. By the time a boy has reached puberty he can manage a plow and a brace of oxen. This places him among men whose essential task is the care of the land. Through types of work and through the sexual division of labor, the child further learns his place in the community.

Children do not indulge in play to any marked extent, although small girls may make dolls of sticks and rags and pretend to suckle them at their childish breasts. Toys are a rarity, although animals, young birds, and insects are collected as pets. Organized children's games are almost non-existent, for children tend to scorn play as babyish. Their ideal is rather to emulate their elders whom they are constantly with, for the mirror of village life is always the preceding generation.

Children do not lack entertainment, however, which is the same as that of their elders. From the time they are infants in arms, they accompany grownups to an evening of storytelling or to a wedding or other gathering. Because of this close sharing in the adult world of entertainment, there is little incentive or opportunity to build a separate children's world apart. Not possessing a separate world or personal solitude, village children lack fantasy, imagination, and personal creativity. This lack of individual imagination is found among adults as well and helps permit the traditional to crystallize and continue.

Sexual knowledge comes gradually to a child in terms of its own observations and age. Mothers and grandmothers handle the genitals of a boy infant in order to sooth him. Masturbation and sex play among children are reprimanded, however. At a young age great stress is laid upon bodily modesty, particularly in keeping the sexual organs from view. This holds true especially for girl children, who are constantly reminded to sit with their legs closed or not to sprawl flat, since that indicates a sexual posture. The words *aib aib* ("shame, shame") or *haram* ("forbidden") are continually reiterated to the child in the training of proper modesty as well as in other forms of behavior. The cult of bodily modesty, including the fuller covering of the body, is observed throughout life.

As a child inhabits the same room as his parents and barnyard life is close at hand, he comes at an early age to full knowledge of sex. His vocabulary soon includes a variety of sexual and reproductive terms, including oaths and jests of a sexual nature. Grownups derive a certain sport from teaching small children sexual words, the meaning of which they are hardly aware, and having them recite them in public. As a child grows up, he learns from precept and later correction that these words are presumably not to be used freely, especially in the company of both sexes. Provocation, however, is accompanied by full license of vocabulary by the child among its own sex as well as in mixed company. The bawdiness and license of language used by all village members is in sharp contrast to the general reserve otherwise observed between the two sexes, and would seem a compensatory measure for the stringent regulations regarding familiarity between the sexes. Speech, rather than action, is a way of cleansing tense atmosphere, while speech in itself is filled with an emotional connotation compensating for the general reserve demanded in adult behavior. Speech at all times, moreover, is the means by which the peasant gives fullest vent to feeling — emotional, aesthetic, or otherwise. This speech possesses vivid imagery and rich metaphor and is concerned with the concrete and the immediate rather than with the abstract and the general.*

A child first learns of the presence of deity through everyday events. The name of God is invoked before the breaking of bread or the undertaking of any important task. God's name resounds in everyday greetings and phrases. God's greatness is proclaimed daily in the call to prayer. Religious holidays and the Ramadan month of fasting further impress upon the child life's tie to God. Boys undergo religious training in the mosque or at school, committing to memory large portions of the Koran. Girls' formal religious training is negligible. Their knowledge of holy writ is gleaned indirectly through village ceremonies and gatherings.

Circumcision is the rite which formally initiates a boy into the religious community. Circumcision also makes a male socially fit for intercourse. The uncircumcised Christian, in contrast, is looked upon as physically unclean. Women, talking among them-

*As Sir Hamilton Gibb has pointed out in *Modern Trends in Islam* (Chicago, 1947), p. 5, "The medium in which the aesthetic feeling of the Arabs is mainly (though not exclusively) expressed is that of words and language. . . ."

selves, mock the dirtiness of the uncircumcised Christian, stating that no decent woman would have intercourse with such a man. Young Muslim men like to brag that circumcision makes a man more potent. But this perhaps is to be related to their general preoccupation with male sexual prowess, which expresses itself as well in jests, greetings, and oaths. Circumcision takes place any time after the first year of life up until adolescence. The small infant is too newly come into life to undergo the ordeal. Group circumcision is the usual method so that the circumciser, called into the village from outside, need only make a single annual visit. Group circumcision, although performed individually in each separate home, tends to impress the rite more strongly on both the individual and the community. Often families have all their sons circumcised at the same time, if age differences are not of too great a span. Following the circumcision, the household may participate in some special dish, while congratulatory sweets are handed to all.

The operation is performed with an old-fashioned razor, the circumciser first solemnly invoking the name of God. Cheers and pious phrases are invoked by family onlookers at the completion of the act. The severed foreskin is then hastily placed in the vent hole above the door, as are the child's first soiled diapers. Having left one condition of life behind and newly entered upon another, the circumcised male, like the newborn infant, is in need of special precaution against the spirit world. The vent aperture connecting the interior of the house with the larger world may be regarded as a symbol of the passage from one stage of life to another, or from the prenatal stage to life itself.

A girl on first menstruating may embrace the large-bellied jar in which flour is stored, so signifying her entry into womanhood and ensuring through sympathetic process her own future status as mother. This rite symbolizes as well her duties as a full grown woman, one of which entails the feeding of a family — bread in itself being the essential foodstuff of peasant life. This is an informal act, witnessed only by her mother. But village women's lives, in contrast to men's, at all times possess less outward and formal manifestations of expression. Women, moreover, form a more distinct world of their own. Their influence and role in the community is covert rather than overt. By being covert, however, it is nonetheless effective.

The world, which lies about a child in infancy and growth and in which, by gradation of steps, he learns his place, is in essential outline the same world within which he participates as an adult. Because this world remains basically the same throughout the life span, tradition is the more easily maintained. The child is faced with no abrupt changes or demands for radical readjustment either during the maturing period or on coming to maturity. The world of adult men and women is merely an enlargement and extension of the world already known. It is the place of kin ties and land ties, both interrelated to religious adherence.

VI

THE WORLD OF MEN

Village men and women form separate spheres. So God formed creation dividing all living kind into male and female. In the village mind this concept is carried over into the inanimate world. Harder forms of rock are described as male, softer, as female; non-bearing soil as masculine, fertile soil as feminine. This sense of consanguinity between man and nature, the attributes of man and the attributes of nature readily projected from one to another or finding a common identity, is found throughout village thinking. Since the stress on the division of the sexes is basic to the Muslim social order, since it exists within the animal order, so it is seen as even part of the inanimate world.

With the onset of adolescence, the division between the sexes becomes more marked in forms of work, social behavior, and spatial freedom. Girls through household chores are drawn increasingly into the sphere of women. Boys through increasing work in the fields are drawn into the sphere of men. This dichotomy of the sexes is basic to the Muslim social order possessing both religious and traditional sanction, the two interfusing. The sense of men and women inhabiting separate spheres persists throughout life and is even continued into the grave, where men and women are not buried side by side, even if man and wife, but each is allotted his sphere or space within the burial ground.

With increasing strength in their limbs and down on their cheeks, growing boys are fully aware of their maturing status and that it is their sex who are the creatures of authority. They tend to isolate themselves from other members of the household, and an older son may try to find sleeping quarters of his own in a shed or storeroom apart from the family room. Growing boys pay increasing attention to their looks and dress, proud of their manhood. They carefully wind their sashes about their waists, douse their heads under pitchers of water, and swagger and loiter about the village store. Alone or in groups they depart for the day to the foothill towns to explore the larger world.

Mothers are extremely lenient towards their sons during this coming to manhood and seem to derive pleasure and pride in watching the young boy mature. Since the son is entering the separate sphere of men, they no longer dare to exercise close authority over him. Father and son, in contrast, may well quarrel during this period. The two are brought closer together as the son takes on a larger share of work on the land. Inevitable bickering rises over the share of the labor, the son resenting the authority of the father, who in turn resents the growing independence of the son and his interest in activities other than work.

Growing boys often take over the greater part of the goatherding. This takes them alone or in small groups from dawn to dusk to the isolated mountain shoulders, a task which adds to the boys' sense of independence. If herding is regularly carried out over a period of years the boy is apt to become surly and uncouth, almost more at home with members of his flocks than with members of the household. Since it is recognized that the task of herding separates the herdsman from the human family, the chore is often given to the wayward son, the dullard, or to the orphan or half-orphan, already isolated from the household center and forced to find what work they can. Shepherd youths serve a number of households and receive pay in a portion of the milk and flocks.

The departure of young men in their late teens or early twenties for a term of venturing in the coastal towns is viewed with general tolerance as are the expeditions to the foothill settlements. It is considered the nature of man that he should explore, just as it is the nature of woman that she should conserve. Animals, it is said, have the same instinct, the male ranging further afield. Besides, by finding work outside the village, the young man earns cash towards the bride-price.

Adolescent boys tend to form cliques or gangs who stroll through the village street at the end of the day. During the pre-marital years of adolescence, the social distance between members of the male sex and the female sex is at its greatest. This is accomplished primarily by restrictions placed on the girl — by confining her close to home and by keeping her under the watchful surveillance of parental eyes. Clandestine courtship or flirtation is strictly forbidden, and what social relations boys and girls have are in the presence of their elders or the girl's family. Since little familiar communication is permitted between the two sexes during these years, close ties between members of the same sex previous to marriage are common. These are often highly charged emotionally, but at best they are looked upon as makeshift relationships which supposedly will terminate at the time of marriage.

Pre-marital chastity is expected of both sexes; it is the strict rule for girls. Deviation from it may bring bloodshed between persons and households. What youths do outside the village, however, and in the cities is not condemned unless it causes reverberation and scandal within the community. It is tacitly accepted that men have their fling in the cities. Young boys who have gone to the foothill towns like to brag to each other and also to their elders that the eyes of the girls were upon them. Adult married men, on returning from similar expeditions, state in the presence of their wives that the women were after them like locusts after corn. It is important to a man at all times that he has a sense of his manhood and that he is the cynosure of other — particularly female — eyes.

Despite the barriers between adolescent boys and girls, opportunities do exist for flirtation and semi-courtship, although these take place in the presence of adults either at social gatherings or during certain kinds of group labor. The long days on the threshing floors when the sheaves are unloaded from the animals, the threshing boards mounted, and the grain winnowed and sieved, provide the opportunity for the close proximity of person to person, for jostling and the inevitable physical contact. House-repairing and house-building provide a similar setting when the young girls hand jars of water to the men for making the mud bricks, or fetch and carry tools. Combined with the work there is jesting and banter, often of a provocative and sexual nature. Under these circumstances, suitable matches may be instigated.

Feast days and the gathering of neighboring households on winter evenings also permit the two sexes to be together. Men take the lead in these social events, but young girls and women, by providing the food, edge in nearer the center of the group. In village dancing, which may be part of an evening's recreation, men and women form their separate groups or lines, the division of life into two sexes being recognized in the dance pattern. But as enjoyment and emotion increase, the two lines draw nearer to one another, almost, but never quite, touching. Herein lies part of the tension and pleasure.

The very fact that there is a well-recognized dividing line between the two sexes engenders an atmosphere of artful intrigue or flirtation in disguise, which in itself provides its own form of village recreation. Young men stand silently on the store verandah and look down on the fountain where the young girls lean to fill their pitchers. The young girls, in their turn, make more trips to the fountain than necessary.

No able-bodied adult remains unmarried, and marriage itself is recognized as much a sign of maturity as the body's physical signs of maturation, the latter demanding the seal of matrimony. Marriage, furthermore, fits an adult into full village society. By mate and offspring, the adult is tied more securely into the kinship pattern and sense of lineage. By house or share of house, by land or by taking on increasingly the care of the preceding generation's land, the adult is more closely tied to locality. Through marriage, an adult adheres to the law of God. Marriage thus enhances and is part of the adult role, giving the individual increasing status since it reflects kinship, local, and religious sentiments. It also serves to promote these sentiments and therefore preserves and strengthens the village as a whole.

Yet men often complain of the burdens of marriage and the new responsibilities it brings into their lives. Were a man to remain unmarried, however, he would lack physical proof of his manhood essential to his self-esteem. He would lack, too, the sense of security that comes through fathering a new generation and of knitting family and land into a visible entity, the two fortifying one another and both related to the continuity of life. Drifting in and out of the village is one example of a man without these ties which give a substance to life. A Turk by origin and a guard on the main highway in former Ottoman days, this man married a woman of the village. She died leaving him no children. Her small share of land was not handed over to her husband since, in village minds, he was never considered a full or true member of the community. Without mate, offspring, land, or kin of his own blood, he remains an anomalous figure, given occasional hospitality by his deceased wife's people. Of himself, he says that life is as bitter as the taste of quinine.

Although man and wife are brought together through the act of procreation, through sharing common living quarters, and through mutual interest in their offspring and in maintaining a living, the cleavage between sexes continues. A couple never shows any demonstration of affection for one another in public. Even within the family circle the relations between man and wife tend to be formal. A man's social life and a woman's social life are carried on mainly between members of the same sex. At the end of a day's work, men seek out the company of their own sex and gather in the coffeehouse, which no woman enters more than momentarily. Men gather at the Friday service in the mosque and in its courtyard for evening prayer. Women pray individually in their homes.

This separation of the sexes in forms of social communication, along with the greater radius of men's spatial freedom, tends to give each sex its own body of knowledge. Men speak disparagingly of women's talk which is concerned with matters peculiarly their own. Women say, on the other hand, that such and such is men's affair and that their sex is not to be consulted. For the sharing of confidences or in moments of crisis each sex turns towards its own members. This being so, significant bonds of personal attachment are not necessary for the success of a marriage, since man and wife, each members of a separate sexual sphere, rely upon the companionship of their own sex.

Man, as father of grown sons, or as grandfather, may retire or semi-retire from the more active work in the fields, handing his land over in all but deed to his mature sons. They, in turn, share part of its produce with him or feed the aging man or aging couple from their family plate. During his later years a man may spend increasingly long hours at the coffeehouse, fingering his conversational beads, engaging in reminiscences, or giving his views on events.

The coffeehouse at all times remains the men's center of communication and a place of informal education. Here youths, mixing with adults and oldsters, are exposed to the accumulated knowledge and experience of all village male life. Here the newspaper is read aloud, or news of events of the outer world is exchanged. Here the guest or sojourner is entertained. Women, in contrast, have no such broad center within which to exchange views. They live largely on hearsay or on recitation of their own doings.

Men in their final years may well be confined or semi-confined to the close quarters of their own home. They sit on the mud stoops beside the doorways, warming their bones in the sun. Old and toothless, they themselves remark that they are much like children, capable of consuming no more than porridge; and it is with children they find their pleasure, amusing themselves with the antics of some small grandchild.

In old age, however, a companionship may grow up between man and wife, not present in the younger years. Conversation between the old man and woman becomes more familiar, resulting in jest and banter and even outspoken tender sentiments. Left much to themselves in house and yard while more active persons are absent, the old couple turn to one another for company or for help in some task.

Sons and their families congregate by the deathbed; sons absent from the village are called home. Over the washed and shrouded corpse is wild keening, proclaiming the glories of the deceased and of the line from which he is sprung. Conveyed to the burial ground on the mountain slope, the deceased is laid side by side with the male ancestors of his line. Over his corpse the *shaykh* proclaims proper holy writ. In death, man is returned to the village soil with which he has had close allegiance. His bones are laid next to his kin, to whom he has felt close loyalty. Through the words of the *shaykh* he rests within his faith and under the oneness of God.

VII

THE WORLD OF WOMEN

The influence of village women cuts deep into village life. In Muslim society it is the male sex which possesses the greater ostensible prerogatives. Nevertheless, back of and beyond the masculine world lies the close-knit world of women, shaping and sustaining village life by indirect rather than direct methods. Men sense this invisible power of women. To old women, in particular, is attributed the power of witchcraft or of the evil eye, both signs of an uncanny force.

The life of the adolescent girl differs radically from that of the growing boy. While the spatial liberty of the boy increases with his years, that allotted to the girl becomes more circumscribed. While the growing boy begins to stand apart from his parents, the maturing girl is kept increasingly under parental surveillance. For the growing girl has the power to disrupt society as a temptation to men.

With other village girls and married women, the girl may roam the higher mountain sides to gather faggots for fuel. Within the village she may take part in the activities of a group composed of both sexes, if married adults are on hand. She may go alone down the street to the fountain to fill the household pitcher. But she never goes unaccompanied outside the village confines or to outlying village areas. When passing alone through the village street or paths, she must at all times conduct herself with modesty, her shawl drawn over her hair, her sleeves to her wrists, her conduct restrained and circumspect. By no means may she loiter to engage in banter with village youths or ever isolate herself with a single man. The adolescent girl has come to sexual maturity, but this maturity has not yet been institutionalized. Herein lies the young girl's disruptive force. No longer a child nor yet a married woman, she stands in a precarious position. There is always the danger that her honor and that of the family may be smirched by some unseemly act by her, or by some man, before she attains full womanhood through marriage and childbearing. No woman, unmarried or married, is ever abroad alone after dark.

The adolescent girl is much with her mother, the two women sharing in all household tasks. While mothers tend to spoil their growing sons, they are increasingly severe with their growing daughters, anxious that they learn to perform all tasks that will fit them adequately for marriage and for care of the home, and more anxious still that they preserve the good name of the family. Although mother and daughter may bicker over small affairs, there is a growing bond of intimacy between them, for both sense their membership within the separate sphere of women, which even within the household forms a domain apart from men.

The father and older brother are the protectors of the maturing girl. They are also the persons who have the ultimate authority over her and to whom she is most beholden. The girl realizes that it is to both that she may turn for aid from offense. At the same time, she realizes she must conduct herself with due propriety if she is to expect protection from the male members of the household. During adolescence and as the growing girl increasingly joins the sphere of women, her relations to the father and brother become more formal and more subservient.

Girls take pains with their dress on feast days, wearing trinkets and new clothing. But in contrast to growing boys, it is thought unseemly for a young girl to lavish too great attention on her looks and dress since this signifies a desire on her part to court the attention of men. Mothers and fathers sternly rebuke the coquettish daughter.

Growing girls, like adolescent boys, tend to form close relationships with members of their own sex or with some young married girl friend who is able to impart to the uninitiated first-hand reports of the intimacies of married life. In contrast to boys, however, girls single out a sole companion, rather than form a group. Two close girl friends may help each other at work, visit each other's homes, and exchange trinkets, in the meantime sharing in one another's confidences. Girls openly demonstrate much affection towards one another and, when in small groups, like to talk about and admire one another's growing bodies. Close girl friends often address each other as *bint al-amm* or "daughter of the paternal uncle," the first cousin on the paternal side being the one who is closest in one's own generation other than members of the immediate family. The term is also synonymous with the "beloved" or "chosen" one, since first-cousin marriage on the paternal side is the preferred Muslim marriage.

Girls marry in their late teens, boys in their early twenties. Parents theoretically arrange a marriage, a *wali* or "go-between" acting in all formal arrangements. The inclinations of both sexes are usually taken into account since it is realized that an amicable household is preferable to one of disputes. Girls confide to their mothers who is the man of their choice. Boys do likewise to both parents.

In the choice of a mate, girls are heavily influenced by the local and kinship factor, since both village and close kin afford a form of security not found in the larger world. Besides, a girl has been brought up from childhood tied close to village boundaries and to village persons, the two forming the world within which she is most at ease. Young men, although influenced by kinship and local ties, may look further afield, preferring a wife from the foothill settlements and thus widening the range of economic ties by fortifying them through bonds of blood.

Girls, in conversation, say they prefer first and foremost the conventional Muslim marriage to the first paternal cousin. This marriage least disrupts the pattern within which they feel most at home. For the first paternal cousin stands next to the brother as protector, while the paternal uncle stands next to the father. The mother-in-law, as aunt of the girl in the kin nexus, may be depended upon for friendly treatment. Parallel cousin marriage on the paternal side, furthermore, removes the girl least from her own

home, allowing her to continue the intimacy with her own mother
and to rely on the protectorship of her father and brother.

The least popular of marriages is when a girl is married into
another village, usually because of economic considerations or
attenuated ties of kin. The girl who leaves her own birthplace
feels bereft of the protection of her family and especially of the
proximity of her mother. She also mourns the loss of the familiar
village scene and setting, which to her has almost a physical relationship.

Wives taken into the village from elsewhere constantly mourn
the rupture from the village of their birth. Squatting on roof tops
at the end of the day, they watch the smoke from chimneys and
hearths of the settlements from which they have come and relate
the activities that are taking place there and of which they are no
longer a part. They make excuses to visit their homes, saying that
it is profitable to exchange crops of the mountain side for those of
the plain. Or they wait longingly until the end of harvest when
their mothers and brothers bring them a small share of home-
grown produce.

These wives who come into the village from outside are grudg-
ingly accepted by the women of the community. They may be
edged aside at the fountain or made to wait longer than their
turn for the use of a communal oven. They are readily blamed
by village-born women for matters not of their making. Men,
more exposed to the larger world, make little social distinction
between the women of the community, whether born within the
village or brought in from outside as wives.

No able-bodied woman remains a spinster, since the unmarried
state is to deny the laws of Creation. The only adult unmarried
female in the village is a woman who has been crippled since birth.
More because of her unmarried position than her disfigurement is
she the butt of jokes, since she does not perform the function for
which she was created. It is said that she sleeps with her *karineh*,
that "alter ego" possessed by both sexes which infests sleep and
dreams and is often considered responsible for a woman's ills, her
outbursts of temper, or illness among her young children. Almost
ostracized by the community in which she plays no essential part,

the crippled spinster lives in semi-isolation with her widowed mother.

Marriage and the birth of a child, especially a son, bring a woman to full sexual and social status. Through childbirth, a woman proves herself an essential part of the kin nexus into which she has married. As housewife, she contributes to the family-land economy. As married woman and mother, she has a definite place within the entire community. Both parents on the birth of the first-born son are addressed teknonymously. The mode of address in itself gives status to a woman, especially. The teknonymous title may even be extended to childless couples as a polite way of overlooking their failure to produce heirs. The *shaykh* of the village and his wife, though not blessed with young, are always addressed as "Abu and Umm Mohammed" (the father and mother of Mohammed) as a title of respect and as a means of glossing over the couple's personal sorrow.

Though wife and mother, however, a woman still adheres to the sphere of women. The prohibitions regulating the activities of a menstruating woman and the general notion that menstrual blood is unclean and capable of defilement are among the causes relegating women to a world of their own. A menstruating woman may not step over the threshold into a house containing a newborn infant, lest the child by proximity be contaminated. Nor may a menstruating woman witness a birth, touch the shroud of a corpse, visit shrines or mosques, or enter a cemetery. Nor, if menstruating, may a woman continue her fast during Ramadan, but is considered unclean for eight days. Intercourse is forbidden during menstruation.

It is at the time of childbirth that women feel most particularly in their own sphere. This is essentially the time of woman's power and an occasion for her own sex, when many village women crowd into the room to share in the event, the part played by men in procreation being all but forgotten. Female voices recite in exhaltation the stories of their own deliveries. In a chorus at appropriate intervals they encourage the woman in labor by cries of "Heave! Heave!" No other occasion in women's lives has the same sense of group cohesion or spirit of common concern. Childbirth is not only the distinguishing mark of woman's sex; it is also her glory, through which new life is given to the lineage, new strength is brought to the village, and God's ordinances are reflected.

The woman in labor half sits, half reclines on goat-skin rugs spread on the floor for the delivery. In her pains she cries for her mother. The mother, though feeling her importance, reminds the daughter that it is still better to call on God. A woman friend sits behind the woman in labor, bracing the latter between her knees. To either side kneel attendant women, the woman in labor tugging on their braided hair as the labor pains increase. Over the woman's up-drawn knees a coverlet is spread. In accordance with the dictates of modesty, however, none of her clothing is taken off and only her long bloomer drawers are drawn down in the final stages of delivery.

The midwife, or woman designated as midwife, kneels before the girl, making appropriate observations beneath the tent coverlet and reporting them to the audience at hand. If the delivery is difficult the midwife may inject her hand into the vagina, first greasing it with sheep's fat; common household scissors are used for the cutting of the umbilical cord. Then the naked child is held aloft, the onlookers in chorus giving thanks to God the Creator from whom stems all life.

Young children of both sexes accompany their mothers to scenes of childbirth. Unconcerned with the process of delivery, they play among themselves. Once the infant is delivered, however, they join in the acclaim, begging to fondle the child and often being permitted to do so. If the delivery is prolonged or especially difficult, a doctor may be called in from the foothill region. But this is a measure only resorted to under extreme conditions and after much consultation between both male and female members of a family. Women with their cult of bodily modesty are averse to intervention by a male doctor. The need to pay a doctor is a further deterrent. The woman after childbirth is tightly bound about the abdomen, rests in bed for several days, and refrains from sexual intercourse for forty days.

The daily meeting place of the village women and a center which they feel is their own domain is at the communal ovens.

The ovens are not only a place of work but a social center and almost a women's club. Here in the semi-subterranean enclosure, hidden from view, all family intimacies are discussed, consolation is found, and endless gossip indulged in. Women taking flight from quarrels with their husbands find shelter in this refuge. Yet the oven interior with its half dozen women and its essential demand for work does not afford the broader social and emotional outlet afforded men by the coffeehouse and mosque. In women's lives there is monotony. There is monotony in being confined not only to village boundaries but also to the round of daily chores which vary less by seasons than do those of men. There is monotony even in the interminable gossip — intensely personal and without wide range. This monotony of women's lives finds its own special outlet through violent outbursts of temper within the closed circle of women. Women's quarrels among themselves are far more frequent than those among men and are accompanied by obscenities, blows, and the throwing of rocks and household utensils. Furthermore, neighboring women often join in, though the affair is not theirs, as if they were glad of an opportunity to break restraints and indulge in unlicensed behavior.

Women are both greater law-keepers and greater law-breakers than men. They adhere to village tradition in forms of dress and general custom more stringently than men. Old women in particular are the repositories of village lore and wisdom. At funerals it is they who through their keening summon up the glories of past village life, reviving and handing them on to younger generations. During birth scenes, they recall their own pangs of childbirth or relate the births of outstanding village members. It is women who are the cohesive factor in a community. Women are the keepers of village medicine, handing down to others their prescriptions and brews. Specific herbs, dried petals of wild flowers, and certain roots and plants are said to have healing powers for both external and internal ailments and are collected and kept by households. Of store-bought remedies and cure-alls, aspirin and baking soda are those most commonly used. Foothill pharmacies and doctors are only resorted to in times of dire emergency or serious accident. Neither the local doctors nor the pharmacies in the region are of high repute, and the peasants have little faith in either. Occasionally, however, trips are made to reputable doctors or clinics in Beirut. Often an ailment is by then too far advanced for cure, and the peasants are likely to hold the doctors responsible for any failures, condemning the medical practices and expenses of the outside world. Local bonesetters are sometimes called in, in case of fractures or sprains. These practitioners are often of herdsmen origin who through the setting of bones in their own flocks have gained a rudimentary knowledge of mammalian anatomy.

Women are more concerned with the world of evil spirits than men are, since their primary function is to rear the tender young whose lives are most endangered by the unseen world. The most common afflictions of children are enteric and respiratory diseases. There is scarcely a household which has not lost one or more of its children in the first five years of life. From infancy on, there is danger of eye infection and trachoma, while skin diseases through lack of bodily cleanliness are common. Although village herbal brews and lotions, as well as occasional store-bought medicines, may be used in doctoring children, these at all times are combined with phylacteries and charms, the more complicated of which are sold by itinerant peddlers. Illnesses may be attributed to natural causes, but, particularly in the case of small children, they are believed to be connected with the malignant powers of evil spirits who have a special predilection for the young. Women, who are the more traditional of the two sexes, have the greater belief in the power of malignant spirits and are the sex which to a great extent keeps alive the traditional village ways.

Women are the conservers of the village. But this conservation reaches beyond custom and law, in which areas women are less strictly conventional than men. A hurried-up marriage, glossing over the awful error of the girl, is arranged by the womenfolk. The theft of money by a young man from his father is concealed by a grandmother, she herself making amends. The primary concern of village women is the preservation of the community. In their own words they say, "We must live." In order to maintain community life, old women in particular work out adjustments by means of covert and scheming methods. These adjustments, outside the boundaries of custom and convention, maintain the village entity through crisis and upheaval.

Older women — those past menstruation and childbearing — have greater freedom than their younger sisters. No longer curtailed by menstrual prohibitions and having performed their essential duties, they have a position of their own where the line of definition between the world of men and the world of women loses its sharp outline. Old women can be bawdy and vulgar in their talk before men without receiving condemnation, since by reason of their advancing years they are no longer identified with sexual activity. They are less modest in action and dress than younger village women. They may even talk back to men and, in the presence of younger men, have authority. Since they are the keepers of the home to which the old man retires, they often gain an upper hand over the man of the house during his declining years.

The world of village women is narrow. In this narrowness, however, there is depth. The force of women is projected through uninstitutionalized rather than institutionalized channels.

Men are regarded as the prime movers of the two sexes — the creators of progeny, the winners of bread, the persons of authority. Yet back of them are the women, who are the main support of village tradition and who, beyond village tradition and convention, stabilize and sustain the village world.

VIII

THE WORLD OF KIN

Kinship, marriage, sex — these are related topics of conversation with which the peasants of Buarij are continually occupied. The division of humankind into male and female is by ordinance of God. The Koran contains injunctions on marriage, incest regulations, and duties of children to parents. The emphasis on bonds of blood and the habit of close kin marriage, particularly on the paternal side, are a part of Muslim tradition.

The small child is called a "bridegroom" or "bride" as a term of endearment. Young unmarried girls confide that they are continually preoccupied with the thought of their marriage day and the delights of love. Youths, working or waiting for the bride-price, grow impatient, and the village wit among them cries "May it rain brides from heaven and each one bring with her her bedding!"

But back of, and beyond, this individual preoccupation with sex and marriage is the deep sentiment that the blood line and lineage must continue. As lineage extends backward into time, so it must continue forward into time. It is in a sense greater than the individual, and within it the individual must play his prescribed role.

The blood bond is the significant kinship factor. The closer the blood ties, the greater the sense of identity between persons, since they partake most closely of the same essence. Blood, moreover, is conceived of as possessing a peculiar import of its own. It is a basic life property. When a new house is completed a cock is slaughtered, its blood dripping over the threshold. Thus the welfare and longevity of the house are assured. At the time of the sheep-slaughter the blood from the animals' throats is poured over household herbs and flowers. Blood is a fertilizer promoting life. At the time of the spring festival girls stain their heels and hands with henna, a substitute for blood and a sign of the renewal of all life. Blood may become contaminated and unclean. Its flow cleanses the body of impurities. Menstrual blood performs this function. Leeching and cupping are means of draining the body of the polluted flow which left to itself can cause illness.

The concept of blood as an essence of life relates to lineage. Blood is extended through inheritance. As a life property it finds new embodiment through successive generations. The male is its chief vehicle and transmitter, just as the male is the dominant sex within Muslim society. Women's blood by reason of menstruation cannot possess the same purity of essence or the same life force.

Blood and land ownership intersect, reinforcing one another. For the peasants of Buarij count their respective lineages from the first male ancestor who came to the mountain side, while previous genealogy is lost track of except for hazy outlines. The present owners of land are not only the descendants of these ancestors, but own and work the land in accordance with close blood ties. As the peasants conceive of themselves as stewards of the land, passing it on from generation to generation, so they conceive of themselves as links in a blood chain, passing on its essence as well from one generation to another.

The village clans or paternal lineages derived through blood from a common male ancestor may, as has been seen, possess certain properties in common such as threshing floors, communal ovens, or a segment of the village cemetery. It is not these properties, however, that the clan regard as their most important asset, but rather the living strength of the clan in terms of total male members and the sum total of land owned by clan members. These two attributes, combined with the past glory of clan ancestors, give a lineage its feeling of importance. The largest clan with the greatest number of adult male members tends to hold the greatest influence in the village, despite the rule that important village offices rotate from clan to clan. Conversely, the smallest clan tends to have least influence.

The importance of the clan to the individual lies in its protective powers. It is the body to which the individual may turn for aid in times of crisis, insult, or injury. It is of greater protective value to the peasant than lesser kin units since it possesses the largest numerical strength. Injury to a clan member by a non-village member or by a member of another clan immediately rallies all clan members together in common concern for a member of the common blood line. A sense of pride and loyalty centers about the clan name, wherein the common pool of blood is identified with a common emotion.

The clan has more meaning for men than for women. This is not only because men are the vehicles through which the blood line is transmitted, but because clan strength is considered in terms of male fighting strength. For this reason the clan with the greatest number of adult males feels an innate strength over the lesser clans of the village.

Women, in contrast, if they have made an inter-clan marriage, have ambivalent feelings towards the clan. Throughout their lifetime they are considered to be a member of the clan into which they were born, but by marriage into another clan they bear children belonging to the clan of their husband. Thus their allegiance is less well-defined and finds orientation in terms of the circumstances with which they are faced. For their own individual welfare they look towards members of their own clan, or more particularly its lesser units — to close paternal kind or to father and brother. For their children's welfare, however, they look to the lineage of which their children are a part.

The cliques formed by village youths often fall into clan patterns, the young unmarried men carrying on banter and verbal rivalry in terms of clan membership. Evening parties during the winter include largely clan members. Engagements, weddings, and funerals always include a full quota of clansmen, though others may be invited as well. The smallness of the village, combined with the linking of clans through marriage, tends to diminish an extreme sense of the clan as a separate entity. Nevertheless, all villagers retain a strong sense of the clan to which they belong, are aware that it is a protective body, and are concerned with preserving its honor and good name.

The clan is composed of joint families and immediate families. No hard and fast rule can be given for the composition of the joint family nor for its exact functions, despite the important role that it plays. The joint family is primarily an economic group banded together for the better welfare of its members or for the better utilization of land. The joint family may consist of a couple and their children who share in an economic enterprise with the paternal grandparents. The couple and their children may share a compound house with the grandparents or live near them. Or two or more couples, married brothers with their children, may set up a similar household. Usually a share of the parent's land is turned over to a man at the time of his marriage. Yet it may prove advantageous for married sons and their father to continue working all land in common, each caring for a specific area but all sharing in the produce. The paternal grandparents may or may not eat from the same common plate as the couple and their children, according to their abilities to care for themselves. The old widow or widower, however, is always absorbed into the household of one of the sons, or moves from son's house to son's house, and is there given care. If there are no sons, the widow or widower is cared for by a married daughter. There is no greater disgrace than to abandon the old.

A number of married sons and their families, especially if living close at hand, may share in the common enterprise of caring for certain of the lands belonging to each. This, however, need not be a permanent arrangement, or more than a seasonal one. The pattern of the joint family and its functions remains at all times fluid. Still, there is a great sense among the villagers that close kin may be called upon to band together for mutual aid whenever the occasion demands. This may entail no more than a single enterprise of short duration. Or again it may be a long-term bond between brothers or between fathers and sons who work land in common for a number of years.

The immediate family inhabits a single room or more of a

compound house, or possesses its own small dwelling. Its members eat from a common plate. The hard cash they earn from work in the outer world or the share of produce they earn as sharecroppers is theoretically considered a family fund. The produce from the family's lands is also its own, unless the family makes some arrangement by which its members work the lands in common with a larger kin group.

Kinship terms are in the main descriptive, differentiating between paternal and maternal kin and indicating degrees of relationship. Kinship terms are used fictitiously. Men and women, and especially growing boys and girls in the village, address each other as brother and sister, irrespective of relationship. For village men are expected to treat all village women as sisters, observing the proper sexual restraints. Women, in turn, should be able to look on all village men as brothers, with the same regard that they have for their true brothers. Persons, particularly old women, talk much of genealogies, describing or placing an individual within his kin framework. The stranger on entering the community is asked to whom he is related, a known relationship helping to establish his credentials. Gossip and talk of persons in the foothill communities are accompanied by reference to kin. That a person should be devoid of close kin ties is almost impossible for the peasant to imagine. To the orphan or half-orphan there is an attitude of pity, since such a child lacks the closest of kin and therefore the background of family and kinship security.

Degrees of relationship, whether on the paternal or the maternal side, define kin obligations and duties. Children are beholden to their parents and they in turn to them. Paternal uncles stand next to the father as the child's guardian and next in male authority over the child. Paternal first cousins stand next to a girl's brother as protectors within her own generation. This close interrelation of persons on the paternal side involving two generations is an intensification of the sense of paternal lineage contracted into a lesser segment — the offspring of brothers possessing the same paternal grandparents, back of whom are the generations leading back to the ultimate ancestor, who is the focal point from which paternal kin sentiments are derived.

In accordance with the degree of distance of relationship, the same general sentiments are projected to other paternal kin, but in diminishing degree. To the maternal kin, except towards maternal grandparents who because of their age are owed deference, a similar set of general sentiments is shown, although lacking the feeling of deep allegiance and the same demand for reciprocal obligations as found on the paternal side.

The paternal lineage or clan prefers to keep itself free from infiltration of other blood. This finds best expression in the conventional Muslim marriage of first paternal cousins. By this system of marriage not only is the blood kept the same through both partners possessing the same paternal grandparents, but also the close allegiance felt between members of the existing generations within the lineage is reinforced and strengthened. In first-cousin paternal marriage, kin on both the wife's and the husband's side of the family are of the same degree of relationship, the sentiments directed towards either side of the family therefore being the same and so establishing an equilibrium and balance. Through marriage of first paternal cousins, land and the working of land remain within a close group of persons bound to one another in allegiance. Through first paternal cousin marriage, furthermore, the stability of the marriage itself is better assured since it is reinforced by the security of close kin bonds and of lands derived from a common source.

Marriages within the village of Buarij are between first paternal cousins (the conventional Muslim marriage), to more distant paternal cousins, to cousins on the maternal side, to individuals of other clans, or to women from outside the village, related or not. Village girls sometimes marry into neighboring communities, usually where attenuated ties of kin already exist. Marriage of first paternal cousins remains the ideal. First paternal cousin families, however, may not possess offspring for suitable pairing in terms of age and sex. The small size of the village, moreover, bringing all persons in contact with one another, tends to diminish the claims of lineage alone and fosters marriage to more distant kin or even between clans. The sum total of inter-village marriages to other than first cousins far outweighs that of marriages to first paternal kin.

While children are still infants in arms, their mothers plan to pair them off in conversation in terms of future marriages. Adolescent girls among themselves list the merits and demerits of village youths. Girls, as it has been seen, aside from romantic considerations, prefer first cousin paternal marriage since it causes the least break with the life they have known.

Marriages of the villagers are to Muslims — to Muslims of the Sunni sect to which the village belongs. No village woman has ever married a Christian. But there have been departures from religious scruples on the part of the man. One village wife is of Shiite Muslim origin, the marriage having come about because the man worked for a long period of time in a predominantly Shiite area. There is still a more irregular departure — that of an aged wife of Christian origin, whose husband took her in partial payment for a debt. The Shiite wife often has her origin thrown at her by bickering women; the Christian wife, however, has fully adapted to Muslim ways. In fact, the religious origin of the Christian wife is rarely spoken of, since that would conflict too radically with village standards. This woman, however, is careful to keep to herself much of the time, despite her long residence in the village.

In village life, ideal behavior is always lauded and kept in view. It is held up as an image to which the community theoretically adheres. But behind this ideal image are inevitable departures, in many cases caused by pressing economic needs. These departures, especially if serious, may be glossed over or not mentioned. By not mentioning them, the village can retain in outward form the concept of village life as dictated by custom and tradition. Silence, as much as gossip, is a form of village control.

The bride-price is a means of stabilizing marriage and establishing a new household through capital investment. It is also a form of restitution for the removal of the girl from her family circle. The bride-price is lowest if a man marries his first paternal cousin, because some consideration is due close kin. Furthermore, first-cousin marriage on the paternal side least disrupts existing kin relations and in fact cements them. The bride-price is highest if a man takes a bride from outside the village, because of the severe rupture the girl and her family have suffered.

The price is in the form of cash or land or a combination of the two. Two-thirds of the price is paid down at the time of the drawing-up of the marriage contract. The remaining third is forfeited if a man divorces his wife. With the cash a woman buys the household furnishings, bedding, crockery, and a large trunk for storage. These possessions, as well as the land, are hers in her own right. Women prefer that the bride-price be in land, or mostly in land, since land is a permanent and productive agency, and is the best guarantee if a woman is left a widow. As women themselves say, "Land abides."

The bride-price is a form of insurance for the girl herself. In a society where prerogatives belong largely to the male sex, the bride-price gives the girl tangible goods to reinforce her position. The tangible property permits a woman to possess a small domain of her own, just as women as a group form a sphere of their own. Lastly, the bride-price stabilizes marriage, since a man is less likely to divorce his wife if on her departure she may take her own tangible goods and receive as well the forfeiture of the remaining third of the price.

The bride-price is an economic transaction. The most pressing and ever present problem of the peasants of Buarij is the making of two ends meet. Elopements, with marriage at the Muslim district court, are not uncommon since the delay in obtaining the bride-price may outwear the patience of the partners concerned. These elopements are in time overlooked by the villagers, for of all departures from village tradition those caused by economic pressures are most easily forgiven. It is known that poverty and continued economic stress can undermine the pattern of village life; but beyond the pattern of village life is the still more needful factor — that life itself must persist.

Under Muslim law, polygyny is permitted up to the number of four wives. In Buarij only one man is polygynous, having, aside from a wife of his own age, a much younger wife taken after his children were grown. The man is the largest landowner in the village. His plural marriage relates to his superior economic status. On the whole, however, the villagers, men as well as women, are opposed to polygyny, not only because of its greater economic demands, but also because of the personal complications it brings into a household.

The drawing-up of the marriage contract is a serious business, with clansmen and neighbors on hand and the *shaykh* reading the appropriate writ. The rite, as with the marriage ceremony, takes place in the home of the girl since she has not yet been legally transferred to her future husband. The marriage ceremony itself is an occasion both for solemnity and for joy. The girl in her bridal outfit sits stiff and unlifelike, just as, during the ceremony, she is taken from one life to another, neither belonging to her former home nor yet part of a new household. The *shaykh* presides, intoning the holy writ. Both the marriage contract and the marriage ceremony are registered at the district Muslim court.

The transferring of the bride and her possessions from her father's house to that of her husband is a high point of the ceremony. The possessions are proudly lifted aloft, all the guests breaking into wild song and cheering, though the mother may weep and beat her breast at the departure of her daughter from home. Even if there is only a short distance to go, the girl rides on animal back — an object of display. The bridal sheets with their stain of hymeneal blood are returned to the girl's family as a token of her virginity. Again blood becomes a symbol of the process of life.

Divorce is uncommon in the village. It is economically impractical because a husband must forfeit the remaining third of the bride-price. Moreover, there is the strong feeling that husband and wife must stay together to provide for the children and to care for the lands and house. Couples often quarrel noisily, and husbands beat their wives cruelly with farm tools or sticks. The unhappy wife may flee to her parents' house for a day or more, but unless incompatibility is extreme, man and wife continue to live under one roof. If the situation is such that neither partner can any longer put up with the marriage, the union may be dissolved even without regard to the payment of the remaining bride-price. If a wife does not produce children, she may be sent home to her parents without further reference to forfeiture of the remaining third of the price, since she is considered not to have fulfilled her prime function in marriage.

Extra-marital relations are known to take place in the village, although on the whole they are rare. These clandestine meetings are said to occur in the farther fields or in the shelter of the higher mountain crags. Theoretically, the adulterous woman deserves death by stoning, in accordance with Koranic tradition, or by being slain by her husband. But such a stringent retaliation has become outmoded because of the growth of district and state law. Often a married woman who is believed to be, or is caught in the act of, carrying on clandestine relations is severely beaten by her husband or is divorced by him. A certain hearty village woman, the mother of seven children, is said to have been found behind a rock with a young unmarried blood of the village; but aside from a severe beating the marriage has continued, since the husband saw no way of providing for the children alone. Teased as a cuckold by men, he continues his family life; and his husky wife, being the stronger of the two, asserts to other women that the beating was without significance.

Amicable couples and young brides and bridegrooms are silent about their affections when in large company. The happy bride and wife, however, confides in her woman friends of the intimacies with her husband, the women comparing their experiences among themselves. Or wives may speak of the general kindness of their husbands who are not averse to helping them carry wood from the high mountain slopes or to sharing in the heavier tasks. Men speak less openly of their affection for their wives. Of sexual relations, they stress their own prowess and capacity rather than the part played by their mates. At all times, men are primarily concerned with their potency and their sexual capacity, which are not only a mark of manhood itself, but relate to their ability to further the blood line.

Attitudes towards kinship, marriage, and sex relate to the concept of the larger life process, which in the peasants' minds must persist above and beyond the individual life of man. The sense of lineage in itself relates to the sense of the continuity of life over and above that of the individual. This sense of a lifeline coincides with that of the continuity and permanence of land since the blood line is founded on the first male ancestor who came to the mountain side. Through close ties of kinship, particularly on the paternal side, both the blood line and the land receive greater protection. Land is necessary to life. Life in itself is the essence of creation. By stressing kinship ties, by knitting person to person in a close fabric of mutual obligations, and by preoccupation with marriage and sex, life itself is better assured, sustained, and fortified by land.

IX

THE WORLD OF WORK

Work is an accepted part of the rhythm of life and is a means of supporting it. The task of providing food and shelter is common to all God's creatures. All persons within the village are drawn into the world of work.

Children begin carrying and fetching as soon as they can stand. Old persons confined to house and yard putter about repairing farm implements and helping in the upkeep of the house. The housekeeping and the care of children are essentially women's domain; the care of the fields and flocks is essentially men's. But between the two spheres of enterprise there is inevitable overlapping in accordance with the size of the task and the number of hands demanded. Women's work has the greater uninterrupted rhythm since it is fundamentally based on the daily round. Men's work has greater variation both in tempo and type since it is fundamentally based on the rhythm of the seasons. Men's work, too, extends into a wider spatial world.

The village working day begins with dawn, when bread is broken for the first meal of the day and the animals are loosed from their night shelters. It ends with sundown and the evening call to prayer, the creeping of shadows being watched to time the return of flocks and men. But persons within the village do not work regular set hours or in terms of continuous unbroken routine controlled by a set time schedule. Rather, the nature of the job at hand dictates the expenditure of time and effort. In the busy season of threshing, the usual day's rhythm may be extended well into the night, the grain being tossed beneath the white light of the moon. In the winter season, work within the village fades off and ebbs except for the routine chores of household and barnyard life.

The peasants of Buarij consider work primarily a means of sustaining life rather than of improving it. Little attention is given to acquiring new mastery over the substances with which work deals. Work is rarely considered in terms of capital gain, by which modes of life may be radically altered. Nor is work thought of primarily as an isolated personal pursuit directed solely towards individual personal ends. Work relates rather to the maintenance of the family or to the larger kin unit through reciprocal working relationships. It relates to the sustaining of the blood line and of life itself — hence to the sustaining of the village community.

In work performance, imaginative enterprise is rare. The village mind, fed by tradition, tends to adhere to the traditional way, although this may not make life easiest or bring greatest profit. Imagination, moreover, where it exists, tends to feed on the past. It does not reach into the future with the aim of radically shaping that future. Nor is there the necessary capital on hand to undertake new ventures. Extreme alteration of working methods, moreover, tends to change the equilibrium of life and to disrupt an established harmony of interests, persons, and needs, long in existence. In his old age, a man will be cared for by his children. This being so there is no need for immoderate exertion. Then, too, there is the land which abides.

Yet the peasants talk much of wealth — who in the general vicinity has more or most, who in the village owns the most land, or who is fortunate enough to possess a brace of oxen. Although there is a certain personal envy, it is not in the peasants' nature to stimulate radical alteration of their own life. They realize, furthermore, that the only method of increasing their incomes on a large scale is to absent themselves from the village for an extended period of time and to find work in more lucrative areas. The migrants to South America have done this, but not always with fortunate results. Others, even entire families, have gone to the coastal area and the cities, sometimes breaking all ties with home. This forfeiture, however, is considered by the majority too great in terms of loss of personal identity with the community and loss of emotional ties insuring security among kinsmen in the place of one's birth.

Women learn working habits from their mothers and so adhere more closely to traditional village ways, since of the two sexes women are less exposed to influences from the outside world. The daily chores of housekeeping, cooking, and making and upkeep of the family clothing extend throughout the year. Combined with these chores is the constant replenishing from barnyard manure of the store of dung cakes for household fuel. In the summer season, work includes as well the preparation of foodstuffs for winter storage. Then there is the family's fat-tailed sheep which must be constantly hand-fed to ensure its conversion into substantial amounts of cooking fat at the time of the autumn slaughter. Women complain that their work is never done, especially during the summer season.

Women's work overlaps that of men. They share in the care of nearer garden plots. They, as well as all village hands, are called into the fields at the time of the grain harvest and threshing. The same holds true during the grape harvest. Women also take part in house repairing and building, mixing the clay and setting the mud bricks to dry in wood frames. But in all joint operations carried on by both sexes, men take the authoritative role.

Men's work is primarily the care of the lands and flocks. The Arab word for "peasant" (fellah) signifies a cultivator of the soil. The plow and the brace of oxen are the signs of the established peasant cultivator. Work in the fields during the busier agricultural season takes men out of their homes from dawn to dusk. During the grape harvest, men often sleep in brush huts in the vineyards guarding their crops, sometimes accompanied by members of their families. Work as sharecroppers on the plain below the village takes men from home for several days at a time, particularly during the plowing and harvest seasons. Here they camp outdoors or put up in shelters provided by the landlords. Young men who act as herdsmen go to the mountain heights for a day at a time or longer during the spring, summer, and autumn seasons. Then there is the winter dispersal of men to the coast land to be herdsmen or to do odd jobs. Men's work, compared to that of their womenfolk, possesses a wider spatial radius, bringing them into greater contact with other men and exposing them to greater variations in tempo and type not only of working pursuits, but also of all activity.

The time of plowing and sowing and the time of harvest demand the greatest number of sustained working hours and the greatest physical effort. Men return from the fields drenched with sweat and weary after the steep climb up the mountain slope from the plain below. This fatigue is lessened first by their womenfolk washing their feet and later by an evening of recreation — card playing, trictrac, or gossip — in the coffeehouse. Yet there are days, aside from the winter season, when there is little or no work on the land. Then men may loaf for long hours or break the spells of odd-jobbing outside the village with the respite of leisure. These periods of leisure and loafing, combined with the wider and more varied activities of their work, give to men's lives a less monotonous texture and context than that allotted to their womenfolk. Leisure is accepted by them as their lot and, during this time, they make no special effort to lighten the burden of the women of the home.

There is little organized recreation during the periods of lightened work or of no work except for the patronizing of the coffeehouse and for the household gatherings on winter evenings. Dancing and feasting are usually reserved for religious holidays, for the drawing-up of marriage contracts, or for marriage ceremonies, although sometimes on a winter's evening a group will break into song and dance to the accompaniment of pipes and drum.

A spontaneous outbreak of joy, except in songs at work, is rare among the peasants. It is dignified and reserved behavior that is lauded, especially on formal occasions. Even small children sit silently at gatherings, one hand folded within the other. However, a pleasure which almost partakes of an activity is derived from the silent sitting in front of doorways at the end of the day.

Throughout the village there is a constant exchange of labor or of payments for labor by a share of the produce. The exchange of labor is greatest among clan members, particularly the segment within the lineage that is composed of adult brothers and their families. Brothers exchange labor in the working of one another's fields. Men who own oxen plow a kinsman's or a neighbor's field in return for a share of the crop. Women help one another in the preparation of winter stores, each complementing the work of the other. As a whole, women engage in reciprocal labor more readily than their menfolk do. The latter, exposed to the conditions of the outer world, may demand cash in return for their services. Although the general trend is for close paternal kin to help close paternal kin, exchange of labor, exchange of crops, or cash payment for labor extend beyond close kin groups and include all households. The common economic needs of all villagers and, before and beyond all else, the basic demands for the necessities of life tend to delete kin divisions in the general pattern of working relations and to unite the village in a single common enterprise, especially at the height of the harvest season.

Although the villagers reciprocate one another in work and exchange or lend tools and household utensils, they preserve a great sense of private property with regard to their land. Quarrels among men, often leading to blows and bloodshed, concern mostly trespass on land, abuse of water rights, or damage of crops and trees. An old woman cries bitterly over the theft of a favorite melon which she has watched flourish and grow. As crops ripen, a tension mounts in the village, each family jealously guarding what is its own.

A similar sense of ownership and pride of ownership exists in relation to livestock. Plowmen are as proud of their oxen as if they were persons and have a warm personal attachment towards them. Women affectionately kiss a milk cow on the nose. Herdsmen have their favorites in a flock. These favored animals have names and are admired and petted. Towards them, as towards land, there is a sense of jealous guardianship.

Yet combined with this sense of jealous possession is a sense of compassion and generosity. Old widows are allowed the gleanings in the fields. A man with oxen gives a day's labor to the plowing of the land of some old couple who have not been blessed with sons. If a peasant loses his grain on the threshing floor through fire or other form of destruction, all households are expected to share in replenishing his stock, since without bread a family cannot live. Life must be sustained beyond all else, thus persons jealously guard that which is theirs and often sleep beside their crops. But since life is subject to the intervention of unpredictable occurrences, to which any man may fall lot, a thread of charitableness and compassion also runs through all work pursuits.

Village tools are on the whole traditional. The plow is not unlike the Biblical plow and, though of ancient origin, is well adapted to the shallow and stony soil. The sickle is of similar ancient origin. The threshing board set with sharp stones or flints is equivalent to the threshing board of Roman times. A few simple hand-operated threshing machines are also utilized, either owned by some village individual who lets out a machine in return for a share of the grain or hired from outside the village and brought in at threshing time.

Both kind and cash are used as mediums of exchange in the village. But it is considered preferable to deal in kind, reserving cash for dealings with the outer world. Wheat is the basic medium of exchange since it can be stored for long periods of time without deterioration, thus providing the basic food staple of peasant diet. All village households exchange varieties of food with one another in order to obtain a mixed diet.

Debt is common among the peasants both in individuals within the village and to persons in the outer world, especially storekeepers. Debts are expected to be paid off after the summer harvest when most produce is at hand or at the end of the winter season when men return to the village bringing hard cash. If money in any large sum is borrowed from persons in the outer world, interest must be paid on the loan. Village members, however, and especially close paternal kin borrow small sums from one another on which no interest is paid.

Men working as sharecroppers receive half the crop in return for the provision of labor, draft animals, and tools. Men working outside the village as plowmen receive a wage either in a portion of the crop or in cash. They themselves prefer cash since it is available at once, while time must elapse before the coming of harvest. All odd jobs outside the village are paid for in cash. In the summer months, foothill villages may hand over their goats to the herdboys of Buarij, since grazing grounds flourish in the higher mountain territory throughout the drier months. Payment for these services is either in cash or in a share of the flock and its products.

During the height of the harvest on the plain, which falls some weeks earlier than that on the higher mountain side, village women as well as men may hire themselves out as paid harvest hands. This money which women earn they attempt to keep as their own. The money which they may earn from the sale of eggs to neighboring villages they also consider their own, since caring for poultry is essentially a woman's task. Women hoard these small amounts of cash, hiding the money in jars or in bedding. Women not only have a sense of their own separate domain, but a sense of preserving their own well-being, which at all times has less individual security than that of men.

By work, life is sustained. Yet work, especially work within the village, is not a separate activity divorced from other segments of village life. The harvest is a backbreaking pursuit as men and women bend over the grain with their sickles and scythes. But it is also a time of much merriment, with all the villagers working in the fields and spending the long lunch hour under the shade of the poplar stand. No person from the village likes to be away from home during these days of full group activity in the open air. Although the peasants show reserve in formal social occasions and are not given to outbreaks of hilarity, nevertheless during periods of working in large mixed groups laughter, song, and banter, also quarrels and obscenities break out freely among them. This is perhaps because the engagement in a common pursuit lets men and women forget temporarily the barriers that otherwise exist between them and, moreover, throws them in close physical contact, which engenders an air of excitement.

As the grain harvest is brought to a completion, "the bride of corn" — a symbolic figure, plaited by the women from sheaves of wheat, which bestows a blessing on household members and the fruit of their labors — is placed over the doorway of the house. The peasant's home, to which the produce of the fields is brought, is equally as important to him as are his lands, the former being the place of the crops' growth and maturation, the latter the place of safe storage. The woman of the house, its chief keeper, has the large key to the door securely tied to the end of her braided hair as she goes about her work. The house, like the land, is property owned by the peasant or his family. Not to own a house or to be obliged to rent one, is considered a disgrace and a mark of inferior status. About the family dwelling adheres a cluster of sentiments, expressing themselves in proverbs and songs of deep emotion. The home is the center of family life, the storage place for crops, and the shelter for livestock — three things assuring security. From the house, persons go forth to work and to it they return.

The family living quarters and the family lands become more and more united as produce is brought in from the fields for the busy time of food preparation and storage. All village members and especially kinsmen are brought closer to one another as they share in work or exchange the produce of their fields. Work, aside from its economic bearing, gives the village cohesion. It impresses upon all village members that the mountain home with its lands, kin, and house, is the place where they are nourished and to which they belong.

X

THE WORLD OF GOD

The peasants of Buarij, as Muslims, sense behind life and within life the ultimate authority of God, to whom all of creation is in final submission. Within Islam itself the sacred and secular aspects of life are interwoven, there being no clear or separate division in many instances between the one and the other. Much of village law and custom stems from or is sanctioned by holy tradition. Inheritance laws, marriage regulations, divorce laws, and the broad outlines of the kinship system with its emphasis upon the paternal line and its stress on the division of the sexes, all have religious sanction. A house may possess no book except that of the Holy Koran. Birth, marriage, and death take place to the accompaniment of proper religious intonations. The name of God finds constant reiteration, in greetings and farewells, before the undertaking of events, and at their conclusion. Because Buarij is a Muslim village that is surrounded by a predominantly Christian majority, the peasants are the more aware of their religious affiliation. This both marks them off from their neighbors and gives to the community a sense of separateness.

Of the Muslim religious calendrical events, only the fasting month of Ramadan and its conclusive feast are observed by the peasants with feeling and with any degree of full village participation. Other and lesser religious holidays may or may not be observed, according to personal inclination. No present village person has made the pilgrimage to Mecca, though many speak longingly of wanting to make the holy journey. An energetic widow with large landholdings and well-established sons is said to horde cash from the sale of crops in the hopes of making the journey as a fitting culmination to her life.

Previous to the commencement of Ramadan, families go on foot to the district center of Zahle to buy new clothes for the occasion and to lay in special supplies for the meal before dawn and for the evening meal, when the daytime fast is broken. On the day before the beginning of the fast, villagers wash both themselves and their clothing, the men indulging in haircuts. Ramadan to the peasants is a time of spiritual cleansing, symbolized by attention to outward cleanliness, while the fast itself is a means of obtaining spiritual purity by handing the body over to God. On the first day of Ramadan a service is held in the mosque, the men attending. Throughout the month the prescribed five daily calls to prayer echo from the turret of the mosque, though during the remaining portion of the year no more than the evening call is rendered, despite religious injunction.

All adult persons within the village, except nursing mothers and women during their menstrual period, hold to the fast. However, if Ramadan falls in the harvest season or in the heat of the year, both sexes often break the fast, particularly that of abstention from water. This breaking of the fast is considered permissible because of the exigencies of life and the need for man to fulfill his duties towards family and land. Intermingled with religious observances is always the greater sense that life at all costs must persist, and that even God in his mercy is in accordance with this outlook.

Children do not begin fasting until the age of seven, since it is realized that youth in all things has its limitations. Nursing mothers do not fast because of the close dependence of a young life on theirs. Children over seven are only asked to fast half a day, but by adolescence the young keep full fast. Often indulgent mothers possessing a single child, particularly a son, do not have the child fast for fear that abstention from food would weaken its life. This is forgiven since a child, particularly a son, is the necessary stay of its parents.

The month of Ramadan is especially propitious for the answering of prayers, thereby renewing the life of man. The twenty-seventh night of the month, or the "night of power" *(lailat al-qadr)*, is the most propitious date of all. Then the doors of heaven are said to open, the angel Gabriel asking grace for every person. Old persons in particular pray for the forgiveness of sins on this night, knowing their lives are advancing towards the realm of God, whose presence is particularly near as the gates of heaven swing wide. Even the trees are said to kneel in reverence on this night lest they look into the face of the Almighty. In Muslim thought there is always the close identification of the secular and the sacred. On the Night of Power it is the sacred itself that suffuses the world, all creation being subject to its rule.

Although religious ritual and ceremony are not strictly observed in the village (except during the month of Ramadan), the men neither saying their prayers nor attending the mosque regularly, the peasants retain and are impregnated with a strong sense of deity and natural piety. This in the main forms an attitude of mind. Village tradition feeds on religious lore as found in the Koran and the Hadith, the sayings attributed to Mohammed. Folk heroes are religious or religious-historic figures, the outstanding caliphs of the past Arab Empire, or figures from the Koran. But behind specific religious adherence and religious tradition, and interwoven with them, is a still deeper and more intimate religious sense that pertains to the more tangible and the more near-at-hand aspects of life, especially insofar as those aspects relate to the problem of maintaining and sustaining life in all forms.

This deeper religious sense may be described as piety, which in Santayana's use of the word, "may be said to mean man's reverent attachment to the sources of his being and the steadying of his life by that attachment. . . . The true objects of piety are . . . those on which life and its interests really depend. . . ."* In the case of the villagers this dependence is on blood ties, land and local ties, and the tie to their faith. This sense of piety subordinates man to the objects or ideals he holds in reverence. Through piety the peasant is subordinated to family ties, to the blood line-

*Irwin Edman (ed.), *The Philosophy of Santayana, Selections from the Works of George Santayana* (New York, 1936), pp. 175-176.

age, to land, and to the larger claims of his faith. Piety is a conservative factor related to that which is already established. Piety relates to, combines with, and enhances the traditional aspects of man's life.

Of considerable influence on the peasant's piety and his attachment to the sources of his being is the persistence of the pre-Islamic nature cults that are incorporated into the general body of village beliefs. On the outskirts of the village against an isolated cliff stands the great oak whose branches are never cut and beneath whose limbs pennies are placed in a cup of rock or candles are lit. The grave of a holy man, or saint, lies nearby. Here, to tree and shrine persons resort at times of crisis to pray and to leave votive offerings. This type of shrine or high place with its sacred tree is a legacy from Canaanite times. But to the villagers it is a close part of accepted and local tradition, all the more efficacious since it stands within and is part of their own local community.

Similar shrines are scattered throughout the foothill area — sacred trees next to springs, to which rags are tied to ward off illness or evil, isolated graves said to contain the remains of holy men, and larger tombs attributed to saints of old. The peasants of Buarij, as well as villagers of the general area, both Muslims and Christians, patronize these shrines, forgetting religious differences in the human concern of finding alleviation for more personal problems. For always underlying the more formal and more institutionalized aspects of life is a deeper stratum of feeling which is concerned primarily with the preservation of life, irrespective of more correlated doctrine. Sacred tangible objects within the known orbit of the peasant's world provide a more intimate solace than the abstract concept of the greatness of God and are a concrete means of reaching out to His bounty. The pre-Islamic, pre-Christian cults persist because they relate to the peasant's sense of piety and the need for the steadying of his life.

Combined with piety, or as counterpart to it, is the belief in evil spirits and the evil eye. These are contrary agencies which may undermine man's attachment to the sources of his being and ultimately endanger his life. Therefore, ritual surrounds the threshold of the house, dispersing evil agencies and ensuring and protecting life, since it is within the home that the acts of procreation, birth, and death take place.

The haunts of evil spirits, demons, and *jinn* are primarily wastelands — mysterious places and areas that have not or cannot be brought under the full subjugation of man. Although the peasant has a sense of piety towards nature and that which sustains him, he also has a fear of those surroundings and natural phenomena which appear unfriendly to him or lie beyond the scope of adequate interpretation or control. A peasant hurrying across a distant field at night protects himself by reciting the first verses of the Koran. He wishes to keep his known world of home and persons and nearer lands as free from the contaminating influences of the hostile world of spirits as his village home is from the intrusion of marauders or hostile persons from outside.

Women cling to the belief in evil spirits and to the body of folk and nature practices more tenaciously than men, who often mock at many of these practices. Women, through child-bearing and child-rearing, feel greater exposure to the capricious agencies of life, and since they do not attend the mosque, they must look elsewhere for support. Village women in times of crisis even enter Christian churches seeking out some saint or relic. Both village men and women often attend Christian feast days in neighboring villages. This is not primarily out of religious interest but because any large feast day, Muslim or Christian, particularly in the more populated communities, takes on the nature of a fair with buying, selling, and entertainment.

Of all the festivities in the year, the spring festival is the outstanding ceremony. In it the peasants' sense of piety finds greatest expression, and in it are combined the basic sentiments of peasant life. The festival is set outside the Muslim lunar calendrical count, since otherwise it would not fall annually in the spring of the year. It is in fact computed in terms of the Christian calendar, its series of increasingly important feast days falling on successive Thursdays preceding Eastern Orthodox Easter Sunday. The festival is a regional celebration participated in by all peasants of the general area, irrespective of religious faith.

First comes the Thursday-of-the-Animals. On this day it is said all animals meet and mate, reproducing their kind. Household working animals are given a rest on this day, while henna, as a sign of blood and life, is dabbed upon their foreheads. Next comes the Thursday-of-the-Plants when unmarried girls, in anticipation of the day that they will become brides, wash themselves in sweet-scented water in which blossoms and wild flowers have been crushed. Young children, as well, are washed in the scented water to ensure their growth and well-being during the year. Next falls the Thursday-of-the-Dead when family graves are visited in commemoration of the departed. Colored hard-boiled eggs are distributed and special wheat cakes baked. Lastly comes the Thursday- or Day-of-the-Jumping, when the inhabitants of Buarij leave the mountain side and troop downward to the plain, where all peasants of the region unite in festival.

On the final Thursday the tomb of Noah situated in a foothill settlement is visited first. It lies in a separate room off a mosque, the raised tomb fit for the proportions of a giant, which peasants say is appropriate since men were larger in ancient days. Here peasants, by touching the tomb or leaving upon it cast-off clothing, receive therapeutic blessing. Near the tomb is a cylinder of limestone, of phallic shape, which persons roll on one another's bodies as a cure and prevention of bodily ills.

Following this, the villagers cross the plain to a place near which the Beirut-Damascus highway enters the Anti-Lebanon mountains. Here on a raised hill is the domed shrine of the Wali Zaur, a legendary local Muslim saint; near the tomb is a well. Peasants and townsfolk within a radius of fifteen miles congregate at this place, coming by overloaded automobiles, trucks, camels, donkeys, horses, horse and cart, on bicycle and on foot. The animals are decked in blue beads and colored garlands for the occasion and the tails of the horses are dyed in henna. Bicycles are wreathed in paper flowers. All persons are dressed in their best garments, varying from out-moded embroidered costumes to smart sailor suits for children. The crowd consisting of some two thousand persons moves group by group into the shrine to receive its blessing of health and well-being. Barren women and those desiring further children seek out the well.

The holy day also takes on the attributes of a fair. Booths are set up on the edge of the plain below the hill or in villages along the main route. Among the merchants and hawkers are the sword dancers, who in frenzy thrust swords through their cheeks with no sign of blood. Soothsayers and magicians inhabit other tents. Along the nearby stream picnics are held. On the level plain take place the horse races, wherein women lie prone on the ground, the horses jumping over them, thereby enhancing female fertility. Then comes the dancing, when the earth, from which wheat is breaking, is stamped and trod in a frenzy by the long lines of men and women.

The spring festival marks the return of life to the land. It marks, too, the return of the peasants who had left their home communities for the winter and the subsequent revival of full village life. The festival with its rising crescendo of holidays is an expression of the reaffirmation of life and of the entire life process. Herein piety is seen in its most basic form as a veneration of the life principle. In the veneration of this principle, lying beyond all doctrine and being a fact in itself, religious differences and local parochialisms are laid aside for the time being. Both Muslims and Christians visit the same tombs regardless of religious designation.

The villagers give no answer to questions concerning the origins of the festival aside from "it has always been so." They make no attempt to explain its meaning except that it falls in the springtime of the year. This same general acceptance is accorded to all ritual and rite. Men, however, see a practical use for the feast day — a time for all local peasantry to gather and exchange news of the year, and report on the state of crops and planting. Furthermore, a peasant looking for work as a plowman or a sharecropper may pick up a job through mingling with the crowd. Women's view differs from that of their menfolk. In their fine dresses, and away from village boundaries, yet secure beside their men, the mingling with the crowds and the atmosphere of semi-abandon acts upon them as a catharsis, liberating them especially from the long closed-in days of the winter. Women, particularly the young girls, speak longingly of the festival far previous to its occurrence.

Though the villagers can give no explanation of the origin of

the feast day and of the crescendo of lesser days, each with its
appropriate rite leading up to the congregation on the plain, the
festival in itself and the lesser rites seem to be related to those of
the ancient Canaanites of the eastern Mediterranean littoral. Their
form of worship was predominantly that of a nature religion, and
their feasts and festivals were primarily designed to maintain the
fertility of the vegetable and animal kingdom. The Tammuz or
Adonis cult of ancient Syria and the Lebanon slopes comes to mind
in the preoccupation of the village girls with the flowers of springtime; while the use of henna as a substitute for blood allies village
rites with the death and resurrection cult of the slain vegetation
god, wherein the flowers themselves bore his blood stains. In the
Thursday-of-the-Dead is seen that ancient Near East belief that
the living as well as the dead form a single community. The veneration of a hillock with its tomb of a holy man and its sacred well
is reminiscent of that early Semitic religious feeling that certain
localities become revered and sanctified as an expression of the
gradual subjugation of nature by man. In the words of Robertson
Smith, "where the god has his haunt [man] is on friendly soil, and
has a protector near at hand; the mysterious powers of nature are
his allies instead of his enemies, 'he is in league with the stones
of the field, and the wild beasts of the field are at peace with
him.' "* This springtime festival is celebrated in varying manifestations throughout the Beqaa Valley, which extends from Syria
through Lebanon into former Palestine.

On returning to the village at the end of the day the festival
atmosphere continues. Dancing is held in the street to the playing
of pipes and drums. Even the outdoor court of the mosque, the
place of ablutions and prayers, is trod by dancing feet. What is
more, men and women break line, members of the opposite sex
dancing shoulder to shoulder.

The spring festival is a fertility rite, each of its Thursdays being
related in its appropriate way to the engendering of life, or, as in
the case of the Thursday-of-the-Dead, to perpetuating the memories of the departed. In the outburst of peasant feeling more

*W. Robertson Smith, *Lectures on the Religion of the Semites* (new ed.;
London, 1894), p. 122.

stringent regulations are forgotten. Life, and its affirmation, is that with which they are concerned.

The spring festival reaches back into nature's order and back of Muslim dogma and doctrine. Yet at the same time, to the peasant it is linked and allied with the sense of deity, since nature itself, and life itself, stems from God the Creator. The sense of piety and the sense of God intermingle in the village mind, the two suffusing the secular. In turning towards God and towards piety the peasants are led by a long-established tradition.

XI

THE VILLAGE WORLD AND THE OUTER WORLD

The peasants of Buarij conceive of their village and its extended lands as their own preserve. The village watchman on his rounds, striding the fields with his staff, keeps an eye cast for strangers or trespassers. Report of any stranger in village territory is immediate news at the coffeehouse. Yet the peasants, particularly the men, except in the dead of winter, constantly go outside the village to the foothill settlements or to more distant areas. But in contrast to these departures, few persons from the outside world enter Buarij situated as it is at the end of a blind road. The village has little to offer aside from its commanding view and flow of fresh waters. Days pass, especially in winter, with no outsider entering the community.

Yet no Lebanese village lives or can live in total isolation, and they all in varying degrees are dependent on the larger world. Peddlers enter the community with packs on their backs or with loaded mules, selling textiles, second-hand clothing, pottery, tinware, patent medicines and phylacteries, cheap jewelry and women's trinkets. The peddlers usually choose the time of year when the weather is most favorable to foot or animal travel and when most persons are collected in the village. The olive merchant makes his seasonal round with olives and oil from the coast land area. With the coming of summer the sheep-sellers move westward from the semi-desert area beyond the Anti-Lebanon range seeking fresh pasturage. To each household they sell a fat-tailed sheep for the summer forced-feeding by hand.

The peddler, the oil merchant, and the sheep-seller, upon whom of necessity the villagers must depend, are long-term acquaintances of the peasants, who trade with the same communities year after year. Between these persons and the peasants traditional relations have been established which ease the transaction of business and permit installment payments or the delay of payment until a more convenient time. A Bedouin sheep-raising family, known to the village for some time, may be allowed to set up its goat-hair tent on village lands paying for grazing rights in flocks, milk products or cash, or a combination of the three. The Bedouin father, however, warns his children not to play with the children of the village lest quarrels break out, the family thereby being forced to move on.

Then there are the less routine peddlers, the itinerant cobbler, the tinker and pot mender, and the photographer carrying his box and tripod. These persons are often of Armenian origin, who, as displaced persons from Turkey, must take to the trades of the road. There is the rare visitor, bearded and foreign in appearance, the scissors-grinder from far-off Afghanistan, who has chosen his trade as a means of making the holy pilgrimage to Mecca. Occasionally a gypsy troop with a dancing bear or a penny-begging monkey pays a call. But gypsies have neither home nor land and are therefore suspect, the village watchman keeping close eye on them. The Afghan scissors-grinder, on the other hand, is welcomed despite his distant origin for he, as a pilgrim to the Holy City, comes in the name of God. The gift of bread is given him to sustain him on his way.

Trucks enter the village at the end of the summer season to buy, for use in coastal market gardens, goat manure dropped in the stables. A mason or carpenter is called in to help with the more difficult bits of house building. Certain villages on the western slopes of the Lebanon range specialize in stone masonry, their men as itinerant stone-cutters and builders travelling the countryside. The occasional stranger comes through making his way on foot or animal back across the mountain paths that spread outwards beyond the end of the village road. A troop of Boy Scouts from Beirut comes to spend the day at the spring. Then there is the local gendarme making his routine call on horseback, and the tax collector coming to sit with the village chief and assess each family's livestock and portion of crop-bearing land.

These visitors are treated in accordance with their mission. No stranger passes through village territory without being interrogated in terms of his pursuit, village of origin, name, kin ramifications, and faith. He himself may stop, or be asked to stop, at the village coffeehouse where he makes himself known and where in accordance with the rites of Arab hospitality he is given coffee and reception. So the peasants themselves expect to be received as sojourners in the larger world, easing their positions as outsiders. The gendarme is treated with crafty respect since he represents the legal forces of the outside world. He is entertained at the village chief's house and also at the coffee shop. The tax collector is treated with veiled contempt, news passing swiftly of his arrival. Arguments, bickerings, and tears among womenfolk ensue as he goes from house to house presenting assessments. He impounds a goat or some household animal of those families who cannot meet the cash tax. As he goes through the street with the collection of animals, kinsmen come forward to make the payment rather than view the harsh sight of households bereft of their possessions and mourning their loss to the outer world.

Aside from the itinerant visitors are the "summerers," or those few families, about a dozen in number, who rent rooms in the village in order to escape the damp heat of the coastal capital of Beirut. These are all Muslims, mostly of the petty shopkeeper class, conservative in outlook, limited in formal education, and many with illiterate wives. Their own limited incomes cause these families to select a simple peasant community; while out of conservatism the men prefer to have their children and womenfolk within an all-Muslim and simple community rather than to spend summers in the more sophisticated resorts or semi-resorts of the western slopes of the Lebanon range, where summer communities are of more mixed clientele. Two of these families, but of superior financial status and background, have bought land in the village and built houses which they have inhabited during the summer season for some dozen years.

Villagers renting out rooms double up with their kin during the two months' visit or sleep in the open air on terrace and roof tops. The Muslim city folk keep much to themselves, erecting awnings about their quarters and terrace space in order to provide privacy, especially for their women. Their children, however, join with the village children in the fields, riding the threshing boards and begging for rides on donkeys. The menfolk of both groups meet at the coffeehouse. Village women and city women pay occasional calls; but a social distance remains between the peasants and the city dwellers. In the case of the families who have bought land and have had a long-term, semi-established connection with the village, relationships are more intimate. Peasant families send a daughter to winter homes in Beirut as a servant, and the city families perhaps arrange medical aid for the villagers or contribute to the rebuilding of the village fountain.

The general attitude towards the "summerers" is one of exasperation rather than an attitude of welcome. The peasants openly state that only economic need drives them into accepting the outsiders. Renting a room is an excellent and easy way of earning hard cash. Little is done, however, to prepare the village for the coming of the visitors aside from cleaning up the refuse along the village street, repairing or building a latrine, or freshening up a room with a coat of whitewash. Village women complain of having to provide farm products to the summer residents and that their presence interferes with their own busy harvest pursuits, despite the cash income derived from the sale of foodstuffs to the visitors. When the summer residents depart there is a feeling of relief in the village. The established order of life can once more be resumed.

Yet there is one economic asset of Buarij — the use of the site as a small summer resort — which could be capable of exploitation. The high altitude, the commanding view, the fresh waters, combined with the village's relative proximity to the main highway and parallel railway, stand in its favor. Younger men of the village who have had most contact with the cities speak enthusiastically of this future. The majority of peasants, however, view the proposition with alarm mixed with disgust. There is the ever-present fear that the outsiders may come to possess a major portion of land, dispossessing the peasants of their rightful heritage. Village fathers and husbands dislike the notion of their womenfolk being exposed to the eyes of strangers. Village women themselves object to the intrusion of an element which disrupts village ways, bringing them and their households in increasing intimacy with outsiders. Yet other Lebanese villages, largely on the opposite side of the range overlooking the sea, increasingly build their economy on the taking-in of summer residents from Beirut. This has proceeded to such a degree that many villages have evolved into resorts with hotels as well as individual residences. But for Buarij, facing eastward and not being part of the more cosmopolitan world overlooking the sea coast, the notion still remains too hazardous.

Relations with the outer world by peasants going out from the village are primarily of an economic nature. These relations include dealings with Christians as well as with Muslims. The sharecroppers work for the most part on the estates of Christian landlords. In the common knowledge that all persons must find means by which to live, the divisive factor of faith is largely overlooked in economic dealings. Still, the Muslim villagers prefer to work for Muslim non-villagers or trade at their shops, since the common denominator of faith is a tie entailing mutual understanding and obligation, and permitting greater leniency in payment of debts or charitableness in terms of work performance. Relations with the outside world tend to be traditional, as are relations with peddlers and merchants who come into the village from outside. Sharecroppers, as well as herdsmen, return to the same lands year after year. These acquaintanceships of long duration tend to obliterate the divisive factor of faith. Upon occasions of crisis when they are in the outside world, however, peasant allegiance is swiftly drawn to persons of their own faith, since it is upon co-religionists that they most depend during their absence from home.

Economic relationships with the outer world inevitably build up social relationships which tend to take on a personal and traditional character. The taking of wives into the village from outside, especially from the nearer foothill settlements, is usually the outcome of, or related to, the peasants' acquaintance with certain persons in a woman's family because of economic dealings. Men, moreover, realizing that the soil of the plains is richer than that of their own mountain side and that work opportunities are greater along the main arteries of communication, find advantage in taking a wife from that region. For though matrilocality is rare, a man taking a wife from the plains may return there with her for portions of the year to find work.

The peasant, alone in new and unknown territory with which he is unfamiliar and where his name is unknown, conducts himself warily. In contrast, large groups of peasants, leaving the village to take grain to the foothill water mill or to work as hired hands on the plain land during the height of its harvest, conduct themselves boisterously and aggressively as they sally forth on their donkeys and on foot. In numbers they feel security. Besides they feel an obligation to display village pride and strength as in a body they enter territory other than their own. They shout loudly the name of the village from which they come, command errant shepherds to remove their flocks from their pathway, and hail and banter each passerby.

The villagers trade part of their own produce with the outside world. The grape harvest is their main cash crop. What is not needed for their own household consumption is sold in a neighboring community which possesses a large grape press serving a wide area. Tomatoes and other vegetables are also sold at the height of the agricultural season. There is as well a small, but steady, trade of goat milk and its derivatives to the foothill communities.

The peasants of Buarij depend on the foothill communities with their wider range of economic interests for a variety of services. Here oxen are taken to be shod and farm tools to be repaired at the smithy; or the small stores are patronized for clothes and household furnishings. Greater leniency in price, in arrangement of part payments, or in delay of payments is expected in dealing with near-at-hand communities than with the world that lies beyond the spatial horizon. The medium of exchange may be either in cash or in kind, although cash is the more usual medium in dealing with the outer world.

Goods and tools bought by the peasants are of both local and foreign origin. Traditional tools intimately related to the peas-ants' lives and in wide use throughout the country are of local output. The threshing boards set with sharp flints are a specialty of western Lebanon, whose slopes of pine forests provide wood for the making of various kinds of farm implements. The heavy stone mortars and pestles come from the lava territory of southern Syria. Most of the pottery comes from a village across the plain, which possesses superior clay pits and specializes in pottery making.

Yet all of Lebanon for over a century has felt the infiltration of foreign goods. The growth of foreign imports, combined with the growth and development of urban centers such as Beirut and the growth of communications, has caused a decline in village crafts. Only the old women in Buarij still handle the distaff, spinning sheep's wool; only a few persons can weave baskets of withes, or plait mats and containers from rushes. The one craft which re-mains, and this belongs to women, is the making of the clay bins for the storage of grain, their rims and sides embellished with raised geometric decorations.

Next to the clay bin stands the empty oil drum, equally serv-iceable as a container. Alongside the household pitcher of clay is the empty kerosene tin bought from the store, both used to bring water from the fountain. Food is prepared over the indoor hearths, especially in wintertime; but kerosene primus stoves are also used, set in the empty hearth or in a convenient corner. All homes are lit by kerosene lamps, although these are used sparingly because of the cost of the fuel. A night wick, consisting of a twisted bit of sheep's wool set in olive oil, may be kept burning. This small flame helps to dispel evil spirits and is the more ef-ficacious since oil, like bread, is considered sacred. Glass windows are the ambition of many, but the majority of homes still rely on closed wooden shutters to keep out the cold. Only one house-hold possesses a raised bedstead and this belongs to the largest landowner in the village. Otherwise all household furnishings remain extremely simple, with all life and living kept close to the floor in peasant fashion. Raised mud-brick benches may line one wall of the house; or there may be a low wooden stool or two. Rush mats, goatskins, and quilts, spread on the earth floor for sleeping, are rolled up and stored in a niche in the wall during the day. Clothing is kept in wooden chests of mountain origin or, more often, in a cheap tin trunk bought by the woman of the house at the time of her marriage. Utensils for the preparation and eating of food form the remaining furnishings and consist of a stone mortar and pestle, a few pottery platters and plates, enamelled tinware, a metal coffeepot, the small cups for offering coffee, and lesser jugs and jars. Not all households possess the large metal caldron for the preparing of the grape treacle and the sheep's fat. This must often be borrowed. Most households possess a rush-bottom chair or two which is always proffered to guests.

The village store contains articles of both local and foreign make. These include local clay ware and also enamelled tinware from England, dried and prepared foodstuffs from Beirut or the district center of Zahle, and sardines from Portugal. There is a shelf of women's trinkets of blue bead amulets of local origin to keep off the evil eye and of cheap plastic jewelry from Japan. There are the local flint wick lighters for men, but also matches from Sweden. This steady, but increasing, infiltration of foreign goods has been going on long enough for the peasants to become accustomed to novel objects displayed in stores or by peddlers.

The selection of goods from the outer world depends on the peasant's economic status, on how much the object harmonizes with village needs and traditions, and on how much the peasant himself has been exposed to influences of the outer orbit. All textiles are of city or foreign origin. But the seamstress hides among her bolts of cloth a flannel print depicting half-naked bathing girls, saying that to display the pictorial scene as outward dress would, indeed, be shameful, though the cloth might well be used as an undergarment for a bride. Women, though utilizing imported textiles, adhere largely to the traditional type of peasant dress with long bloomers to the ankle and tight-bodiced dress, of almost equal length, with sleeves to the wrist. Always their heads are shawled. The strong cult of bodily modesty combined with the feeling that there is a proper costume by which the peasant is identified deflects them from readily adopting city or Western dress, except for an occasional factory-made sweater or high-heeled shoes used for social occasions. A woman, moreover, should never be conspicuous, setting herself up for the attraction of others' eyes. A sewing machine is owned by the village seamstress and is also the treasured possession of a few other women. The machine is adapted for a sitting position on the ground. Almost all the women's and children's garments, and most of the men's, are cut and sewn within the village.

Men, in contrast to women, are less controlled by the demands of modesty, both bodily and individually, and are more exposed to the direct contacts of the outer world. On return from sojourns to the coastal areas they often bring with them trousers of European cut, odd jackets, and European shoes. This clothing they usually save for social events or for visits to the outer world. For work they tend to revert to the wearing of voluminous trousers, wide belts, and collarless blouses. This costume is a sign of their mountain origin. To abandon it altogether is disloyalty to the village home or a sign that a man thinks he is too good for the community.

Younger men adopt items of Western dress and wear them more frequently than older men. It is part of their preoccupation with personal display in their first years of manhood; also it is important for them to show that they have been to the towns. All men wear heavy winter European overcoats of secondhand origin replacing the former goat-hair mountain cloaks once made in the villages.

Young girls are less conservative in their dress than their mothers and make attempts to adapt the peasant dress to more Westernized modes, doing away with the tight bodice. As for their coiffure, though retaining the two long braids, they cut short the front portion of their hair. Many of the older women bear tattoo markings either as a blue dot on the forehead between the eyebrows or as geometric designs upon the wrist or back of the hand. These body markings are regarded for the most part as purely decorative, although an occasional woman says they help to ward off evil. The custom has been entirely given up among young women and growing girls, women themselves saying it belongs to "olden times."

While working, both sexes wear heavy mountain slippers or sandals made from old automobile tires. Young women, particularly, cherish a pair of high-heeled shoes for social events and for excursions outside the community. Usually they put these on just before entering a town, hiding their mountain slippers under a convenient stone. They say that these shoes give them a feeling that their lives are not all work and that they are on a holiday excursion.

New techniques, new objects imported from the outside world, improvement in communciations, particularly car and train service, new economic opportunities such as road-building, and more frequent and longer visits in the larger towns inevitably broaden the horizon of the village world and dilute its adherence to tradition. Young men, in particular, gather in the coffeehouse to talk of political unrest or of the national and larger Arab setting.

Yet at one and the same time the peasants continue to consider their village as an entity peculiarly their own. This point of view is derived from a strong set of personal sentiments interwoven with the feeling that the village affords the best guarantee of security, although this security is not necessarily based primarily on economic factors but on the allegiance of person to person. The close bonds of kin, particularly within the paternal blood line, establish a fabric wherein the individual at all times is certain of some form of aid and assistance. From kin, from known persons, and not from the larger impersonal world, may human response to human needs be expected. The personal and human element is the larger since there are no highly developed techniques which intervene between persons or isolate person from person. The village world is the place of greatest security because land, with its recurring crops, is possessed. In the outer world there is not this sense of possession of durable and fertile property. Towards land and house there are the interrelated emotional bonds of personal, kin, and ancestral sentiments. Interwoven with kin and local sentiments is the sentiment of piety combined with religious faith.

The sentiment of piety tends to fix other sentiments and to fix village tradition. An equilibrium is achieved through the interrelation of kin, land, and religious ties. This interrelationship gives the village a static rather than a dynamic quality.

Within this equilibrium, which is static rather than dynamic, centripetal rather than centrifugal, there is a quality of strength — strength in maintaining the village sense of integrity and strength in facing and opposing the outer world. This quality of strength is all the more tough since it is rooted in and fed by deep-seated emotions. To the Arab, these emotions are as much a part of reality as are elements of the objective world and are fused with, and part of, the pulse of village life. The Lebanese Arab Muslim village of Buarij possesses a hard core and kernel — as does all the Arab world. This kernel has its own peculiar vitality. The core is not, and cannot, be easily demolished. It persists by reason of the depth, the interpenetration, and the interlocking of sentiments.

Date Due